Leadership Meta-Competencies

Leadership Meta-Competencies

Discovering Hidden Virtues

DIMITRIS BOURANTAS and
VASIA AGAPITOU

Athens University of Economics and Business, Greece

Routledge
Taylor & Francis Group

LONDON AND NEW YORK

First published 2014 by Gower Publishing

2 Park Square, Milton Park, Abingdon, Oxfordshire OX14 4RN
52 Vanderbilt Avenue, New York, NY 10017

Routledge is an imprint of the Taylor & Francis Group, an informa business

First issued in paperback 2020

Gower Applied Business Research
Our programme provides leaders, practitioners, scholars and researchers with thought provoking, cutting edge books that combine conceptual insights, interdisciplinary rigour and practical relevance in key areas of business and management.

British Library Cataloguing in Publication Data
A catalogue record for this book is available from the British Library.

Library of Congress Cataloging-in-Publication Data
Bourantas, Dimitris.
   Leadership meta-competencies : discovering hidden virtues / by Dimitris Bourantas and Vasia Agapitou.
      pages cm
   Includes bibliographical references and index.
   ISBN 978-1-4724-2068-8 (hardback) — ISBN 978-1-4724-2069-5 (ebook) — ISBN 978-1-4724-2070-1 (epub)
   1. Leadership—Psychological aspects. I. Agapitou, Vasia. II. Title.

   HD57.7.B68 2014
   658.4'092–dc23

                                                                              2014011277

ISBN 13: 978-1-4724-2068-8 (hbk)
ISBN 13: 978-0-367-67009-2 (pbk)

Contents

List of Figures	*ix*
List of Tables	*xi*
About the Authors	*xiii*
Acknowledgments	*xv*

1 From Leadership Competencies to Leadership Meta-Competencies 1

Introduction	1
The "Being" of the Leader: Trait Approach to Leadership	1
What the Leader Has To Do and How: The Behavioral Approach	2
Transformational Leadership	4
Ethical Leadership	5
Authentic Leadership	7
Spiritual Leadership	9
Servant Leadership	10
A Synthesis of Leadership Theories: A Systemic Approach	11
The *Raison d'Être* of Leadership: What the Leader Ought to Achieve	12
What Leaders Ought to Do and How: The Leadership Behavior	13
What the Leader Ought to Be	14
Leadership Meta-Competencies: The Hidden Virtues of Leadership	16
Concluding Thoughts	19

2 Leadership and Existential Thinking 21

Introduction	21
The Need for a Paradigm Shift	22
A Philosophical Turn	24
The New God	26
So, What is Existential Thinking?	27
Meaningful Motivation	32
The Need for Mindfulness	36
Mindfulness and Leadership: An Attainable Link	38
Resilience	39
Concluding Thoughts	42

3   **Phronesis**   **45**
     Introduction   45
     Ethics   48
     Values from Ancient Eastern and Western Philosophy   52
     Defining the Aristotelian Phronesis   52
     The Eastern Perspective   55
     Modern Phronesis   56
     Phronesis as a Leadership Virtue   62
     Phronesis and Self-Awareness   63
     Phronesis and Humility   64
     Phronesis and Authenticity   65
     Concluding Thoughts   66

4   **Character**   **71**
     Introduction   71
     The Value of Character in Leadership   71
     The Definition Problem   72
     Character is …   73
     Traits   74
     Values   74
     Virtues   76
     The Ten Virtues of a Cross-Enterprise Leader   78
     Character Development   80
     How Character Develops   81
     Concluding Thoughts   86

5   **Integrity**   **89**
     Introduction   89
     In Search of a Definition   89
     Integrity as a Virtue   95
     Integrity in Leadership   95
     Organizational Outcomes   98
     Concluding Thoughts   100

6   **Solitude as a Leadership Meta-Competence**   **105**
     Introduction   105
     The Concept of Solitude   108
     The Generic Benefits of Solitude   109
     Solitude as an Enabler of Effective Leadership   112
     Solitude Enhances Self-Awareness   113
     Solitude Facilitates the Leader's Envisioning   115

Solitude Helps the Leader's Focus and Commitments 116
Solitude Enhances a Leader's Learning 117
Solitude as an Enabler of the Right Thinking 118
Solitude Enables Cognitive Resilience 122
Solitude as an Enabler of Ethical Leadership 122
Solitude and Connection with Others 125
The Practice of Solitude 126
Solitude as a Leadership Meta-Competence 129
Concluding Thoughts 130

7   **The Issue of Trust**   **131**
Introduction 131
The Meaning of Trust 132
The Benefits of Trust 133
Trust Building: The Main Work of the Leader 139
The Origins of Trust: Integrity, Ability, and Benevolence 140
Building Trust within a Team and an Organization 145
There is No Organizational Trust without Socially
        Responsible Leaders 148
The Virtuous Circle of Effective Leadership and Trust:
        Bringing it All Together 150
Concluding Thoughts 152

8   **Developing Leadership Meta-Competencies as**
Organizational Traits   **153**
Introduction—From Individual Traits to Organizational Traits 153
The Meaning of Organizational Culture 154
The Organizational Culture as a Source of Competitive
        Advantage or Disadvantage 157
The Leadership Culture 162
Shaping the Leadership Culture 164
The Leader as Leadership Culture Creator 165
Leaders Develop Leaders 170
Discovering and Developing the Hidden Values of the Virtues
        is a Leader's Responsibility 173
The Lifelong Learning Journey 173
Concluding Thoughts 178

Index   *179*

List of Figures

1.1   Leadership as a system   11

1.2   The *raison d'être* and the accountability of the leader   13

4.1   Kolb's experiential learning cycle   84

7.1   Definitions, levels, and outcomes of trust   151

8.1   Criteria for leaders' evaluation in General Electric   169

8.2   How to transfer culture   170

List of Tables

1.1   What leaders do: The roles approach to leadership behavior   3

1.2   List of the most frequently used competencies   15

4.1   The six virtues and the vices   77

4.2   Good and bad outcomes of presence or absence of virtues   79

6.1   Generic benefits of solitude   110

6.2   The positive effects of solitude experience on leadership   113

6.3   The main benefits of solitude   127

6.4   Emotions that arise before, during and after the solitude episodes   128

6.5   Events that trigger the solitude episodes   129

7.1   The benefits of trust for leaders   134

7.2   The benefits of trust for teams   136

7.3   The benefits of trust for the organization   138

7.4   How leaders gain the trust of their followers   145

7.5   How leaders build trust among team members   146

7.6   How leaders build trust in the organization   147

About the Authors

Dimitris Bourantas is a Management and Leadership Professor, Head of the Executive MBA and MSc in Human Resources Management at the Athens University of Economics and Business. He has written seven best-selling books. He has also published articles in internationally acclaimed scientific journals and supervised PhDs that have been awarded European prizes. Bourantas has acquired substantive professional experience, having worked as an executive, consultant, and trainer for a large number of Greek and multinational companies, including: Citibank, Coca Cola, Nestle, Unilever, Diageo, Nokia, Oracle, Rank Xerox, Pepsico, AIG, Roche, Credit Agricole, and Pfizer. He specializes in the development of leading executives and teams, change management, company culture management, and the strategic alignment of companies and organizations.

Vasia Agapitou has a BSc in Psychology from Panteion University of Social and Political Sciences, Athens and an MSc in Work and Organizational Psychology from the University of Hull, where she won the Tom Hoyes prize. She is currently researching strategic leadership and existential intelligence at Athens University of Economics and Business. She also lectures at the Business College of Athens. Agapitou has practised as a psychologist and her experience includes working at a center for the rehabilitation of torture victims. She has authored one book.

Acknowledgments

We would like to express our gratitude to a number of people who helped us with this book; to all those who provided support, talked things over, read, wrote, offered comments and assisted in proofreading and design.

We would especially like to thank Nancy Papalexandri for her valuable insights on the content and title of the book.

Also, we wish to thank Kleio Akrivou, Shenjiang Mo and Evi Papalois who co-authored with Professor Bouranta a paper on solitude, as appeared in the *Journal of Business Ethics* (2011), which has been a great inspiration for developing the concept of solitude. Also, we would like to thank Ourania Kardasi and Panagioti Kampisiouli for helping us with the chapter on solitude and Iasona Anagnostopoulo for his great suggestions.

Special thanks to our families who supported and encouraged us throughout this journey.

Reviews of
Leadership Meta-Competencies

Professor Bourantas and Vasia Agapitou build upon the voluminous academic literature on leadership to introduce the concept of leadership meta-competencies and to explore six that every great leader must possess. More importantly, they show how these personal competencies can be converted into organizational traits, something that can be the basis for sustainable competitive advantage. This is a wonderful book, firmly grounded in the academic literature and full of useful and surprising insights. It is destined to become a standard reference book for any future studies on leadership.

Costas Markides, London Business School, UK

The book is an important contribution to leadership development since it manages to combine Aristotle and Plato with the most current knowledge, and also identifies meta-competencies as the foundation of effective leadership behaviour. As such, it is an indispensable guide for those who wish to ensure authentic, ethical and transformational leadership in action.

Nikos Koutsianas, Co-founder and Managing Director, Apivita, Greece

Chapter 1

From Leadership Competencies to Leadership Meta-Competencies

Introduction

The existing literature on leadership is immense and, to a great degree, inconsistent, confusing, and not integrated. Scientists from various disciplines such as psychology, sociology, philosophy, anthropology, history, management, and political sciences, pose questions and try to give answers to various issues from different points of view. At the same time, several practitioners describe their experiences and suggest rules, principles, and methods which most of the time come in the form of a prescribed recipe. Even the definitions of leadership amount to thousands. So, one, just from these first few lines without even having to go deeper into studying the phenomenon, can easily abide by the highly cited paradox as articulated by the great leadership scholar James Burns: "while the leadership is the most widely studied phenomenon at the same time it's the less understood." So, since with this book we aspire to contribute to a better understanding of leadership, we believe that prior to introducing the definition and importance of leadership meta-competencies, it is important to acquaint the reader with the most popular, useful, and influential theories that seek answers to the fundamental issues of leadership, namely emergence and efficiency.

The "Being" of the Leader: Trait Approach to Leadership

The focus of the earliest studies on leadership was mainly on physical characteristics and personal traits of the leaders. Research efforts orientated toward answering the question of why some people were leaders and some others not, or to put it differently, which are those traits that distinguish the leaders from the non-leaders? Obviously, there is nothing wrong with the question there; on the contrary, apart from appealing to our curious nature, it can provide us with some useful and applicable insights. But, the way the question has been approached has led to the creation of a long list of personality traits within which some of them appear controversial to each other or lack objectivity. Moreover, the theory does not manage to explain adequately the many leadership failures in spite of the required traits. Besides, this approach has been criticized for not taking into consideration either the conditions or circumstances under which leaders operate nor the work they are called upon to accomplish.

Despite all these, the question concerning "the being" of a leader or which traits and skills must a leader possess in order to be effective and successful is absolutely essential given that the emergence, selection, and development of leaders depend upon the given answer. That is actually the main reason that we observe a renewed interest from part of the academic community in the previous few years concerning this initial approach to leadership. Researchers, having at their disposal more rigorous and sophisticated statistical methods, investigate the traits of leaders in relation to leadership behavior and effectiveness, assuming that what we do depends upon who we are.

Furthermore, the trait approach is developed around the idea that people occupying managerial positions have a strong impact on the culture, ethos, and general atmosphere of the organization. Indeed, it has become rather safe to suggest that by selecting the right people, organizational effectiveness will be increased. On top of that, trait approach may serve as a means for self-awareness and as a development tool; by evaluating their own traits, managers can gain an idea of their strengths and weaknesses. Currently, the research on this approach considers traits as a precondition for effective leadership. Following this line of thinking, we argue that some of the elements that constitute the *being* of leader, such as character, morality, and motivation, are of crucial importance in the quest of a consensual leadership model.

What the Leader Has To Do and How: The Behavioral Approach

The second approach to leadership, chronologically following the trait approach, puts the emphasis on the leader behavior or the *doing*, thus placing it at the other extreme of the aforementioned line of research. Shifting conceptually away from the leader as a person toward the leadership process, the basic assumption here is that anyone who adopts the appropriate behavior can potentially become an effective leader. In short, the behavioral approach attempts to answer two fundamental questions: firstly, "what should the effective leader do?" and secondly "how should they do it?"[1] The questions are approached through the establishment of the roles that account for the effective leadership behavior. Some indicative answers are then presented in Table 1.1, derived from Mintzberg,[2] Quinn et al.,[3] Kouzes and Posner,[4] and Senge.[5]

At the same time another stream of research, namely the situational or contingency leadership theories, seeks to decipher the most effective leadership style (ranging from autocratic to participative and people-oriented to task-oriented) taking into consideration the situation, the followers' maturity, the task at hand, and the relationship between the leader and the followers. What is useful and needs to be kept in mind from these theories is the acknowledgment of the fact that a singular ideal leadership style applied in every situation is not only utopian but also wrong; instead, the appropriate leadership style is dependent upon the particularities of each case, which the leader ought to judge correctly and then adapt the leadership style accordingly.[6] In other words, it is required that the leader possesses an armory of traits from which they select and adopt the ones that the situation demands and from there exhibit the appropriate behavior in order to correspond to the situational contingencies.

Table 1.1   What leaders do: The roles approach to leadership behavior

Mintzberg (1994)	Quinn et al. (2007)	Kouzes and Posner (2007)	Senge (1990)
Figurehead	Innovator	Model the way	Designer
Leader	Broker	Inspire a shared vision	Teacher
Liaison	Producer	Challenge the process	Steward
Monitor	Director	Enable others to act	
Disseminator	Coordinator	Encourage the heart	
Spokesperson	Monitor		
Entrepreneur	Mentor		
Disturbance handler	Facilitator		
Resource allocator			
Negotiator			

1   House, R., & Adity, R. (1997). The social scientific study of leadership: Quo vadis? *Journal of Management*, 23(2), 409–473.
2   Mintzberg, H. (1994). *The Rise and Fall of Strategic Planning*. New York: The Free Press.
3   Quinn, R.E., Faerman, S.R., Thompson, M.P., & McGrath, M. (2007). *Becoming a Master Manager: A competency framework*. New Jersey: John Wiley & Sons.
4   Kouzes, J.M., & Posner, B.Z. (2007). *The Leadership Challenge: How to keep getting extraordinary things done in organizations* (4th edn). San Francisco: Jossey-Bass.
5   Senge, P. (1990). The Leader's new work: Building learning organization. *Sloan Management Review*, 7–23.
6   Bass, B. (1985). *Leadership and Performance beyond Expectations*. New York: The Free Press.

Although the theory is supported empirically and is predictive due to the methodology employed, it fails to explain leadership effectiveness in various situations.

In the last decades, ahead of the new challenges in the organizational environment (that is, complexity and the pressure for constant change), the search for the most effective leadership style has evolved to produce a series of interesting theories that take into account the need to learn, adapt, and balance the multiple stakeholders' different interests. The following chapters discuss some of the most influential and widely-accepted theories of our era.

Transformational Leadership

The transformational theory has been developed to meet the needs of organizational learning, continuous adjustment and change, creativity, innovation, reinforcement, and human development. It can be regarded as a continuation of the charismatic leadership theory, according to which, the leader's perceived charisma was the source of inspiration and group concession by emphasis on expectations, self-sacrifice, and performance beyond the call of duty.[7] The transformational leaders' influence is based on four components or roles, namely, idealized influence, inspirational motivation, intellectual simulation, and individualized consideration.[8]

By using an idealized influence, leaders demonstrate confidence for a better future, create individual and collective meaning based on common vision and mission, and set high standards of moral and ethical choices and behavior as well as high performance standards. Their performance and actions are exemplary as a result of living their own life guided by clear values and beliefs. These leaders place the collective and their followers' interests before their own which they are also willing to sacrifice for the sake of the organization. The followers admire, trust, and respect the leader and collectively identify with the vision, mission, goals, and performance standards. The inspirational motivation means that the leader speaks to the followers' higher needs, guides people toward self-fulfillment, enhances their confidence, self-esteem, hope, and optimism, enables them to participate in decision making and problem solving and, finally, motivates them in

---

7　Rafferty, A., & Griffin, M. (2004). Dimensions of transformational leadership: conceptual and empirical extensions. *Leadership Quarterly*, 15(3), 329–354.

8　Bass, B., & Steidlemeirer, P. (1999). Ethic, character and authentic transformational leadership behaviour, *Leadership Quarterly*, 10(2), 181–217.

becoming powerful. Through intellectual stimulation, the leader renders followers able to truly and deeply understand the need for change, look at the big picture, evaluate a situation, challenge assumptions, question the status quo, and take initiative. Furthermore, they stimulate creative innovation and out-of-the-box thinking and help people change mindsets and paradigms that don't work and to see old things with new glasses. The last parameter, that is individualized consideration, means that leaders develop and cultivate a unique form of communication with every single follower, treat them according to their personality, expectations, and needs, and invest time in teaching, coaching, mentoring, and other developmental activities so that they grow, flourish and prosper.

Both the academic community, as evidenced by the extensive citations and empirical studies, and leadership practitioners have made the concept of transformational leadership very popular in recent years. So, for example, transformational leadership has been empirically linked to increased employee satisfaction, organizational commitment, satisfaction with supervision, extra effort, decreased turnover intention, organizational citizen behavior, and overall high employee performance. Furthermore, research on the antecedents of transformational leadership has found that locus of control and conscientiousness, optimism, moral reasoning, intelligence, and emotional intelligence[9] are some of the factors that determine the emergence and application of the theory's premises. However, it should be noted that the theory has not been accepted wholeheartedly, as can be seen in the arguments which question the theoretical basis of transformational leadership. Amongst the criticisms made, the most significant ones focus on the dubious validity of MLQ—the instrument used to test the theory— on the accusations of transformational leadership being an "elitist" concept and on the ambiguity of measurement criteria.

Ethical Leadership

A second theoretical concept that has received considerable attention in recent years is ethical leadership and, as its name suggests, it places morality and ethics at the heart of its conception and evolvement. In its more simplistic description, ethical leadership specifies how leaders "ought to behave." A more generally accepted definition is "the demonstration of normatively appropriate conduct

---

9   Bommer, W., Rubin, R., & Baldwin, T. (2004). Setting the stage for effective leadership: antecedents of transformational behaviour, *Leadership Quarterly* 15(2), 195–210.

through personal actions and interpersonal relationships and the promotion of such conduct to followers, through two-way communication, reinforcement, and decision making." Ethical leaders communicate ethics and values, visibly and intentionally, by their examples and role modelling to influence followers' ethical or unethical behaviors. They use rewards, punishment, and discipline to keep followers committed, principled, and accountable for ethical conduct. They are characterized by integrity; they "walk the talk" or abide by what they preach; are honest, fair, and principled decision makers; and they are caring toward broader society. They are guardians of common good and motivated by altruism.[10]

However, ethical leadership has also been the subject of severe criticism. Eisenbeiss, for example, agreeably noted that the above description of ethical leadership appears to be rather vague as it fails to specify any particular norms ethical leaders can refer to. Therefore, drawn from Western and Eastern philosophy, religious traditions, and theories of leadership (such as transformational, authentic, spiritual, and servant), she proposed a model that identifies four essential normative reference points of ethical leadership— the four central ethical orientations.[11] Eisenbeiss calls the first ethical orientation *humane* and means to treat others with dignity, respect, compassion, charity, altruism, love, and to see them as ends, not as means. The second is the *justice* orientation and relates to issues of fairness, non-discrimination and favoritism, respect for diversity, equal treatment of others, and taking fair and consistent decisions. The *responsibility* and *sustainability* orientation refers to the leaders' long-term views on success and their concern for the welfare of society and the environment. This orientation is rooted in a new leader's sense of responsibility for the community and may be expressed by a long-term focus on organizational performance, reflection upon the impact one has on society and the natural environment, and the consideration of the interests and needs of future generations. The remaining central point around which ethical leadership should be judged, according to Eisenbeiss's model, is called the *moderation* orientation and it includes the notions of self-mastery, self-control, temperance, humility, harmony, and the Aristotelian golden mean (the middle point between extremes—one of excess and the other of deficiency). In reality, it refers to finding the balance between legitimate organizational objectives and/or stakeholder interests.

---

10   Brown, M., & Trevino, L.K. (2006). Ethical leadership: A review and future direction. *Leadership Quarterly*, 17(6), 595–616.
11   Eisenbeiss, S. (2012). Re-thinking ethical leadership. *Leadership Quarterly*, 23(5), 791–808.

Although ethical leadership is a construct still emerging in the leadership literature, it has received considerable attention following the Enron case and other recent ethical scandals in business, government, sports, non-profits, and even religious organizations. This attention is manifest in the diversity and nature of the research conducted in the field, as exemplified for example by the number of studies investigating the antecedents and the positive outcomes of ethical leadership. The main antecedents positively related to ethical leadership are the leader's character, values, and personality traits, such as agreeableness, conscientiousness, moral reasoning, internal locus of control, and self-monitoring. As far as positive outcomes are concerned, the most important are the contagious effect on followers' ethical conduct and decisions, trust in the leader, the resultant employees' satisfaction, commitment, and motivation, and the attributable diffusion of ethical culture and climate throughout the organization.[12]

Authentic Leadership

Authentic leadership has been explored sporadically as part of modern management science, but found its highest levels of acceptance since Bill George's 2003 book *Authentic Leadership*. The theory is based on the concept of authenticity which was developed early on by the ancient Greek philosophers (now called "self-awareness") and later on by the modern philosophical movement of existentialism. Socrates refers to authenticity with the term "self-inquiry," meaning that an "unexamined" life is not worth living. The basic element of authenticity is "to be yourself" (that is, acting in accordance with and in consistence with one's true self, values, beliefs, and thoughts). Based on the review of literature, Kernis and Goldman[13] propose four key components of authenticity: awareness (that is, awareness and trust in one's thoughts, feelings, motives, and values); unbiased processing (that is, objectivity and acceptance of one's positive and negative attributes); behavior (that is, acting in accordance with one's values, preferences, beliefs, and needs rather than acting to please others); and relational orientation (that is, achieving and valuing truthfulness and openness in one's close relationships).

---

12 Trevino, L., Butterfield, K., & McCabe, D. (2001). *The Next Phase of Business Ethics: Integrating Psychology and Ethics*, Emerald Group Publishing Limited, 3, 301–337.
13 Kernis, M.H. & Goldman, B.M. (2006). A multicomponent conceptualization of authenticity. In M.P. Zanna (Ed.), *Advances in Experimental Social Psychology* (pp. 283–357). San Diego: Elsevier Academic Press.

Out of several definitions on authentic leadership, the following may be one of the most representative ones:

> We define authentic leadership in organizations as a process that draws from both, the positive psychological capacities and a highly developed organizational context, which results in both, greater self-awareness and self-regulated positive behavior on behalf of the leaders and their associates, fostering positive self-development. The authentic leader is confident, hopeful, optimistic, resilient, transparent, moral/ ethical, future oriented, and gives priority to developing associates into leaders themselves. The authentic leaders do not try to coerce or even rationally persuade associates, but it's rather the leaders' authentic values, beliefs and behavior that serve as a model for the associates' development.[14]

Authentic leaders are "genuine people who are true to themselves and to what they believe in. They engender trust and develop genuine connections with others. Because people trust them, they are able to motivate others to high levels of performance. Rather than letting the expectation of other people guide them, they are prepared to be their own person and go their own way. As they develop as authentic leaders, they are more concerned about serving others than they are about their own success or recognition."[15]

As a theoretical construct, authentic leadership is relatively new and as such it lacks extensive empirical evidence. But, the theory has turned out to be rather attractive and intriguing to a great part of leadership scholars, a fact that is evident by the amount of studies trying to establish correlations with other concepts, or investigating the antecedents or the outcomes of authentic leadership behavior. So, for example, it has been found to positively relate to the notions of hope, optimism, resilience, ethics and moral identity.[16] Accordingly, research has identified a variety of positive outcomes that derive from exercising authentic leadership, such as establishment of trust in the leader, increased levels of job satisfaction, organizational commitment, empowerment, work engagement, and high standards of job performance. However, there

---

14 Luthans, F., & Avolio, B. (2003). Authentic leadership development, in K. Cameron, J. Dutton, R. Quinn (Eds), *Positive Organizational Scholarship: Foundations of a new discipline* (pp. 241–261). San Francisco: Barett –Koehler.

15 Gearge, W., & Sims, P. (2007). *True North: Discover your authentic leadership.* San Francisco: Jossey Bass.

16 Gardner, W., Cogliser, C., Davis, K., & Dickens, M. (2011). Authentic Leadership: A review of the literature and research agenda. *Leadership Quarterly*, 22(6), 1120–1145.

have been some voices that warn the academic community about the dangers lurking when accepting a concept that has received so much popularity so quickly. So, for example, in spite of the frequent reference to the existentialist tradition (for example, Heidegger or Sartre) and authenticity, the central idea of the theory is not analyzed meticulously based on the referent philosophical tradition but instead the focus is on how authenticity can be a vital addition to a leader's toolkit in order to increase efficiency.

Spiritual Leadership

With the dawn of the new century, the forces for societal and organizational change press for a more holistic approach to leadership that integrates all the aspects of human existence, namely body, mind, heart, and spirit. Fry,[17] assuming that a learning organization comprised of open, generous, reflective, and empowered employees serves this paradigm transformation better than a centralized and bureaucratic one, developed a theory of spiritual leadership. He defined it as comprising the values, attitudes, and behavior that are necessary to intrinsically motivate one's self and others so that they have a sense of spiritual survival through calling and membership. This entails:

- Creating a vision wherein organizational members experience a sense of calling in their life as meaningful and as something that makes a difference. The vision creates a broad appeal to key stakeholders, defines the destination of the journey, reflects high ideals, establishes a standard of excellence, and encourages hope and faith.

- Establishing a social/organizational culture, based on altruistic love, whereby leaders and followers have generated care, concern, and appreciation for both self and others, thereby producing a sense of membership and being understood and appreciated. The altruistic love is defined as a sense of wholeness, harmony, and well-being produced through care, concern, and appreciation for self and others. It is based on traits and qualities such as forgiveness, kindness, integrity, courage, trust, and humility.

Fry further adds the variable of faith/hope in his model; he argues that if people are driven by faith, which he defines as the "conviction that a thing unproved

---

17 Fry, L. (2003). Toward a theory of spiritual leadership. *Leadership Quarterly*, 14(6), 693–727.

by physical evidence is true," then they are characterized by certainty in their pursuit of their goals and on their way to achieve them. In his own words, "spiritual leadership proposes that hope/faith in the organization's vision keeps followers looking forward to the future and provides the desire and positive expectation that fuels effort through intrinsic motivation"[18] (p. 714). However, although the theory is promising, there are a couple points of criticism—the first is about the strict distinction between spirituality and religion and the second about the poor validity of the empirical studies studying spirituality or spiritual leadership.

Servant Leadership

Servant leadership is a theory first introduced by Greenleaf[19] based on the natural feeling that one wants to serve. Then, conscious choice brings one to aspire to lead. This idea stands away from some modern conceptualizations of leadership, according to which the choice to serve follows the choice to lead. This difference is evident in the manner the servant leader takes care of other people's needs; they make sure that other people's highest priorities and important needs are being served. Much research has been conducted on servant leadership; Dennis for example developed the Servant Leadership Assessment Instrument. Patterson thought of servant leadership as a logical extension of transformational leadership theory, defining servant leaders as "those who lead an organization by focusing on their followers in such a way that the followers are the primary concern while the organizational concerns are peripheral."[20] In her model, Patterson includes seven virtuous constructs that define servant leaders and further shape their attitudes and behavior. So, servant leaders 1) demonstrate agapao (love), a Greek term that refers to moral love; 2) show humility, in a sense that they are egoless, warm and human; 3) are altruistic, which is defined as helping others selflessly, just for the act of helping, with personal sacrifice; 4) are trustworthy; and 5) are of service to the needs of others. It has been argued that the servant leadership framework is not easy to embrace mainly due to the reluctance of leaders to give away personal power and become servants. However, the model presumes development, flourish, and growth for the recipients of the acts of a leader who is strongly and intrinsically directed toward serving others.

---

18 Ibid., 714.
19 Greenleaf, R. (1996). *On Becoming a Servant Leader*. San Francisco: Jossey-Bass Publishers.
20 Patterson, K. (2003). Servant Leadership: A theoretical model. *Dissertations Abstract International*, 64(2), 570.

A Synthesis of Leadership Theories: A Systemic Approach

After having briefly introduced the main leadership theories, in this chapter we attempt to combine them through a systemic approach (Figure 1.1). Accepting that leadership can be viewed as an open system presupposes that it possesses some of the necessary conditions in order to be classified as such. So, we assume that leadership is an open system because it is characterized by an assemblage of parts whose relations are interdependent, the boundaries between the parts are frequently amorphous and ever-changing, and it needs resources from the environment in order to survive. To be more specific, every system is thought of as having inputs which, after having being processed somehow, result in altered outputs. In leadership, the inputs can be the traits, skills, knowledge, and everything that answers the question "how should a leader be?" This stage of the process includes the leadership roles, styles, and different types of behavior that answer the question, "What is a leader expected to do and how?" The leadership outputs are not always obvious, tangible, or easy to measure, since they are not explicit performance targets but instead result in employee motivation, esteem opportunities, values creation, and all those ideas that constitute the reason for being (*raison d' être*) of leadership.

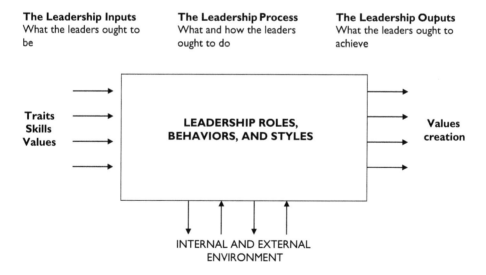

The Leadership Inputs
What the leaders ought to be

The Leadership Process
What and how the leaders ought to do

The Leadership Ouputs
What the leaders ought to achieve

Traits
Skills
Values

LEADERSHIP ROLES, BEHAVIORS, AND STYLES

Values creation

INTERNAL AND EXTERNAL ENVIRONMENT

Figure 1.1   Leadership as a system

The *Raison d'Être* of Leadership: What the Leader Ought to Achieve

Leadership, by definition, aims to obtain results. Today's leaders are expected to get results right and to get them right fast. We have high expectations of our leaders and want them to deal effectively with various and complex circumstances while at the same time establishing sustainable success for the future. What's more, they are expected to be victorious by managing intelligently the constantly emerging problems; in fact, their intelligence should be high enough to overcome their equally highly intelligent counterparts from other competitive organizations.

All these expectations seem to imply that leaders play a significant role in the organization valuation. Indeed, leadership is responsible for accurately assessing the value of the organization, judging which dimensions are the most important for determining company value, and evaluating an organization's long-term prospects for success. Now, if the constant creation of value is the prerequisite for the lasting success of any organization, then it is safe to argue that value creation is the *raison d' être* of leadership. Taking this thought a little further, we might say that one of a leader's roles is to balance the oftentimes competing interests and needs of the various stakeholders, that is, employees, customers, investors, and broader society. So, for example, leadership must ensure the continuous satisfaction of the organization's customers through a competitive value proposition, which among others includes charging fair prices for products or services, standing behind the quality of products or services, and providing courteous customer service. At the same time, leadership is expected to protect shareholders' rights and ensure competitive return on short and long-term investments. Furthermore, leaders are bound to treat the employees fairly and respectfully, satisfy their basic and higher needs, and offer them a physically and socially safe workplace. Lastly, leadership should promote the general welfare of the local communities and broader society by protecting the environment, offering sustainable economic development, protecting human rights (for example, by eliminating child labor), and getting actively involved in programs supporting social needs. Now, that's a hard job, isn't it?

As logically follows, achieving these results presupposes that leadership safeguards and promotes high standards of quality, innovativeness, adaptability, and competitiveness by offering and seeking constant learning opportunities and facilitating change inside the organization. But, these organizational competencies largely depend upon the fundamental

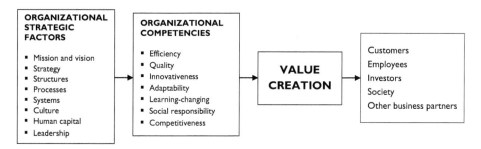

Figure 1.2   The *raison d'être* and the accountability of the leader

parameters that compose the "being" and define the "becoming" of the organization such as mission, vision, strategy, structures, systems, processes, culture, human capital (intellectual, emotional and social), and leadership as an organizational trait, elements that require securing the main accountability of the leaders in all the hierarchical levels. According to this approach (see Figure 1.2), leaders are expected to achieve balance and results—both short-term and long-term—and continuously serve multiple constituents. This further implies that they are accountable for the "being" and "becoming" of an organization which is competent in creating value for today and for the future. These leaders' accountabilities are very well expressed by Collins and Porras with the metaphor of "time teller" and "clock builder."[21]

What Leaders Ought to Do and How: The Leadership Behavior

When the results and the responsibilities of the leaders are set clear, the next question that logically surfaces concerns the way these responsibilities are supposed to be accomplished. To put it differently, what are the definitive characteristics that constitute efficient leadership behavior? There are two important points in this question—the first one has to do with the definition and meaning of leadership behavior and the second is related to the characteristics that render leadership behavior efficient. In order to approach the first issue, we need to consider what results the leader is expected to achieve results-wise and the means at their disposal in order to achieve them. Now, if we wanted to elucidate the main aspects of leadership, the first aspect would be the attainment of results and the second the creation of a future perspective for the organization through continuous learning, development,

---

21 Collins, J.C., & Porras, J.I. (1994). *Built to Last: Successful habits of visionary companies.* New York: Harper.

and adjustment. These aspects can be achieved through two different kinds of means: the human factor and the non-human assets such as strategies, structures, processes, systems, methods, tools, and so on. Based on these two dimensions and by combining the aforementioned theories and approaches, we can approach the content of leadership behavior in terms of the specific roles they have to develop.

The efficient exercise of these roles requires two fundamental functions on behalf of the leader; the first one is the ability to judge correctly, make proper decisions, and communicate them to the rest of the organization. The second question concerns the ability to diagnose the contingencies of each situation and then adopt the leadership style that is most appropriate; in this quarry the situational leadership theories offer a relatively normative and practically useful framework. However, it is should be noted that the various contemporary leadership theories, namely ethical, transformational, and authentic, define and emphasize some generic characteristics that are positively linked to the effective leadership behavior such as authenticity, morality, humanity, humility, and meaning creation, which must be evident enough in order for the followers, peers, and others to perceive and identify them.

What the Leader Ought to Be

The last aspect of the leadership open system regards the question of what leaders ought to be in order to perform their roles and maintain an effective leadership behavior and style. The most prevailing approach is related to leadership competencies. The rationale behind this approach is that the leadership behavior consists of roles and functions which in turn require specific effective behavior that can be further developed. According to this approach, the selection, evolution, and leaders' development lie upon the competence model that each organization sets according to the nature of its transactions, vision, size, strategic plans, culture, and challenges posed from its environment. Table 1.2 presents an extensive list of competencies resulting from a brief survey that took place in a variety of organizations. As far as the development of those leadership competencies concerns, apart from the traditional training methods, a series of other techniques have been proposed, such as coaching, mentoring, and 360-degree feedback.

Table 1.2   List of the most frequently used competencies

• Job knowledge	• Building team
• Accountability for results/focus	• Managing performance
• Dependability	• Developing people
• Customer focus/commitment	• Respect for others
• Execution	• Self-confidence
• Flexibility	• Impact and influence
• Relationship management	• Courage
• Business knowledge	• Charismatic leadership
• Initiative/speed	• Individual consideration
• Problem solving	• Intellectual stimulation
• Creativity/innovation	• Respected player
• Communication skills	• Strategic influencer
• Integrity/ethics	• Strategic conceptualizer
• Performance management	• Acts wisely and decisively
• Talent development	• Ensures alignment
• Staff management	• Support the business, stand behind successes and failures
• Business management	• Bias for action
• Direction setting	• Technical competence
• Change management	• Emotional intelligence
• Passion	• Systems thinking
• Leadership	• Problem solving/decision making
• Judgment	• Global perspective
• Focus	• Intellectual capacity
• Gets results	• Business health and results
• Teamwork	• Vision and strategy
• Learning, self-development	• Building alliances
• Inspiring and motivating people	• Organizational ability
• Planning and organizing	• Maturity and judgment
• Continuous improvement	
• Networking/relationship building	
• Strategic vision	
• Values communication	
• Commercial drive	
• Building organization capability	
• Creating the future	

Although the approach of leadership through the notion of competencies has been extensively employed, there is a number of recent studies arguing that this approach to leadership and the relevant learning development activities do not provide sufficient explanation of the leadership effectiveness, especially now that the latter is given wider meaning in the recently developed conceptions of transformational, authentic, and ethical leadership. But, as in all matters, it all depends on the vantage point; so, this lack of sufficient explanation of leadership effectiveness has set the foundation of re-conceptualizing and studying leadership in a much wider sense following the general tendency in sciences which promotes the universality at the expense of specialization.

Indeed, this tendency has given rise to a much more fruitful quest for personality traits which lie behind the specific skills and competencies such as character, values, and wisdom. Apart from that, there is also another point that adds up to the above argument and regards the self-leadership issue—the existing literature on self-leadership maintains that the development of skills and competencies and other personality traits (such as resilience, grit, and humility) is the responsibility of the leader themselves.

Leadership Meta-Competencies: The Hidden Virtues of Leadership

From the preceding brief review of the most important leadership theories, it is apparent that we have at our disposal the theoretical knowledge and methodology to approach to a satisfactory level the three main questions that comprise the leadership phenomenon. These questions are interrelated— meaning how we answer one of them effects the way we answer the others. So, what the leader ought to achieve and which behavior to display in order to achieve the prescribed results all depend on who the leader is in terms of traits, knowledge, skills, abilities, or competencies. It is important to note that the questions are of equal value, but nevertheless need to be answered in a progressive order. That being said, this book attempts to answer the third question for two reasons: first, because of the vitality of the leader's "being" in determining the efficacy of leadership behavior, roles, and functions and, through them, the leader's results;[22] second, prior to this book, the question has not been sufficiently answered, at least not to the degree that the other two questions have.

Even if someone is not familiar with the leadership literature or practice, the previous succinct presentation of the theories perhaps suffice to infer that the list of the proposed leadership skills and competencies is very long. These skills and competencies are considered prerequisite for the effective exercise of leadership, meaning that they are tied to leadership roles, functions, and the appropriate leader style and behavior.[23] Each organization selects from this long list the elements that are considered more useful to the assessment and development of the leadership potential taking into account the vision, mission, and nature of activities, desired culture, strategies, challenges, and

---

22 Wright, T.A., & Goodstein, J. (2007). Character is not "dead" in management research: A review of individual character and organizational-level virtue. *Journal of Management*, 33(6), 928–958.

23 Munford, T., Campion, M., & Morgerson, F. (2007). The leadership skills strataplex: Leadership skills requirement across organizational levels. *Leadership Quarterly*, 18(2), 154–166.

the particular characteristics of organizational environment. Based on these, the organization hires, shapes the succession plans, develops, produces, and rewards its leaders.

Competence (or competency) is the term that describes the ability of an individual to do a job or a task successfully. It is further described as a set of defined behaviors that provide a structured guide enabling the identification, evaluation, and development of the behaviors in people. Some scholars see competence as a combination of practical and theoretical knowledge, cognitive skills, behavior, and values used to improve performance; or as the state or quality of being adequately or well qualified, having the ability to perform a specific role. For instance, life management competency might include systems thinking and emotional intelligence, and skills in influence and negotiation. Leadership competencies are considered as basic leadership building blocks that enable people to become more effective leaders. On the other hand though, although the approach of competency model can be very useful, it only grasps a small part of the whole spectrum of effective leadership behavior; indeed, this approach seems to be the "tip of the iceberg" since it leaves unanswered at least four more essential and practically useful questions that lie under the surface of the sea.[24]

First, given the cognitive and behavioral complexity of the leadership behavior and the fact that leaders, as all individuals, are an entity that bring their whole personality to work, the question that arises concerns the nature of the relation between the particular leadership skills or competencies that will ensure the consistency, cohesion, and harmony among each other and from there ensure the whole of the leader. Effective leaders are not a sum of a set of competencies, however long or broad the list. Effective leaders come in all sizes and shapes, with a tapestry of strengths and weaknesses that they apply in complex combinations to get the work of the organization done. One possible way to approach this question is to hypothesize that there are some other overarching competencies or traits that are necessary for the development of additional ones. For example, the self-awareness and the learning competence may derive from another series of leadership skills, competencies, or traits which are higher hierarchically.

Second, Boyatzis points out that leadership competencies address the issue of "what a person is capable of doing and what have they done in the past

---

24 Hollenbeck, G., McCall, M., & Silzer, M. (2006). Leadership competency models. *Leadership Quarterly*, 17(4), 398–413.

but not what they will do." In other words, the competencies alone are able to explain and describe how we perform but fail to provide us with any insight on the reasons we perform that way. Therefore, it is necessary to comprehend the intention of the reason, the will, and desire that give rise to these competencies in order to develop and enhance them.

The third issue is related to the unilateral persistence from part of the academic community to research the issues that relate to the positive side of the leadership phenomenon. But, apart from the common knowledge that we all share, research findings have come to confirm that our understanding of situations happens through polarities, meaning that by focusing on the bright side we simply overlook the dark. It doesn't mean that it does not exist. Specifically on competencies, there have been some scholars suggesting that for every competence there is its counterpart, an incompetence. For instance, McCall notes that the team player is not a risk taker and also lacks independent judgment; the innovative may be unrealistic, impractical, uneconomical, and idle while the analytic thinker may be led to paralysis by analysis, is afraid to act and is inclined to accumulate big piles of things.[25, 26] The question thus needing to be asked is: "Are there certain competencies or traits which ensure harmony that enhance the bright side while confronting the dark side of the leaders' competencies?" For example, what could ensure the balance between interpersonal competencies and the strong drive for results?

The fourth issue that also served as an initial motivational factor for undertaking this book concerns the case where the combination of two or more competencies or a cluster of traits can be viewed under a more holistic approach. In other words, can we argue that the combination of competencies give rise to another competence or virtue which is different from the total obtained by the mere addition of its components? If we take, for example, the notion of integrity, we can see that following the code of ethics or always going by the letter of the law (components of integrity) does not suffice to call someone a person with integrity.

All these previous issues have led the recent quest of building and expanding the current leadership competencies models in order to account for situational and outcome variables in explaining why a leader can be effective in some situations and not others, as well the reasons why leaders develop and correctly

25 McCall, M. (1998). *High Flyers: Developing the next generation of leaders.* Boston, MA: Harvard Business School Press.
26 Judge, T., Piccolo, R., & Kosalk, T. (2009). The bright and dark sides of leaders' traits: A review and theoretical extension of the leaders trait paradigm. *Leadership Quarterly,* 20(6), 855–875.

use their competencies. Although not explicitly articulated, it is in fact a quest about the hidden virtues of the leaders. And the word hidden has two meanings here—firstly, it connotes those virtues that cannot be considered clairvoyant and, secondly, because they have been left buried for quite some time at the expense of the quest of more specific characteristics. So, for example, wisdom, character, values, ethos, and existential thinking can explain, at least to a large degree, the current leadership competences development and emergence, and the leader's integration into a whole, as well as being the components of the cross-situational leader's generic traits and desired leadership outcomes.[27, 28, 29]

We argue that the quest for these questions leads to the notion of meta-competencies. The prefix meta- denotes those competencies that operate on a higher level and from which other competencies or virtues are generated. In the same manner, Reynolds and Snell use the term "meta-qualities" in order to describe those qualities, namely creativity, mental agility, and balanced learning skills that reinforce other qualities. Several authors use the term "meta-skills" and "meta-competences" to identify certain key competencies that overarch a whole range of others and are prerequisite for developing other skills.[30]

In accordance with the above argumentation and the questions that constitute the essence of leadership presented earlier, we propose that the term "meta-competencies" can define the leader traits or competences that meet at least three criteria. First, a meta-competence is the synthesis of several skills and personal traits that together shape up into a different whole or competence. Second, from this different whole derive a set of competencies that can be further developed; at the same time, it can also serve as the compass for the right use of other important competencies. Third, it is generic across different situations and across time.

Concluding Thoughts

To recapitulate, we argue that the notion of leadership "meta-competencies" can contribute to a better and deeper understanding of the leadership phenomenon

27 Quick, J., & Wright, T. (2011). Character based leadership, context and consequences. *Leadership Quarterly*, 22(5), 984–988.

28 Hannah, S.T., & Avolio, B.J. (2011). Leader character ethos and virtue: individual and collective considerations, *Leadership Quarterly*, 22(5), 989–994.

29 McKenna, B., Rooney, D., & Boal, K. (2009), Wisdom principle as a meta–theoretical basis for evaluating leadership. *Leadership Quarterly*, 20(2), 177–190.

30 Reynolds, M., & Snell, R. (1998). *Contribution to Development of Management Competence*. Sheffield: Manpower Service Commission.

in terms of emergence, development, and efficiency, since it forms the basis upon which a number of other leadership competencies are being built. Based on the existing bibliography we consider that such critical leadership "meta-competencies" are the leader's existential thinking, integrity and character, solitude, phronesis, and the development of trustworthiness. In the chapters that follow, we present in detail each of these issues and we further discuss the leader's traits and competencies that emanate from them.

Chapter 2

Leadership and Existential Thinking

Introduction

Well begun is half done…

Among the thousands of books written on the definition and meaning of leadership, and the ensuing diversity of opinions, there is a general agreement that leadership is a process of some sort of influence between one individual, the leader, and a group of people, usually addressed as followers. In addition to that, what distinguishes leadership from other forms of influence is that the leader draws on some form of authority, power, or control. Furthermore, if we wanted to take a deeper look at the main scope of leadership literature, we would realize that it has traditionally been focused on rational empiricism, wherein only phenomena amenable to knowledge through direct experience were given attention. That focus further implies that certain aspects of the leadership phenomenon, such as emotions, character, personality, and intellect were neglected at the expense of a more tangible and results-oriented approach.

However, in the last two decades, there have been calls for leadership theorists to explore the inner person or the innate ideas of the leader. As follows, a number of scholars have responded to that call by proposing and elaborating on several elements that are essential for effective leadership. So, for example, effective leadership is conditioned to credibility,[1] emotional intelligence,[2] character,[3] ethics,[4] and spirituality.[5] The list of the elements has

---

1. Kouzes, J.M., & Posner, B.Z. (2007). *The Leadership Challenge: How to keep getting extraordinary things done in organizations* (4th edn). San Francisco, CA: Jossey-Bass.
2. Goleman, D.P. (1995). *Emotional Intelligence: Why it can matter more than iq for character, health and lifelong achievement*. New York: Bantam Books.
3. Burns, J.M. (1978). *Leadership*. New York: Harper & Row.
4. Ciulla, J. (2004). *Ethics, the Heart of Leadership*. Westport, Connecticut: Praeger.
5. Fry, L.W. (2003). Toward a theory of spiritual leadership. *The Leadership Quarterly*, 14(6), 693–727.

grown big over the years, but there sits a problematic; leadership practitioners have treated and used them as recipes for success. Putting it differently, those essential characteristics were not seen as potential areas to be cultivated but instead as techniques that would create a favorable view of the leader and the organization, thus resembling more the job description of an image-maker. To make our point clear, ethics cannot be integrated into strategy by proclamation. People or institutions do not become more ethical just because they incorporate ethics in the company's mission statements, long-term strategic plans, public pronouncements, or codes of conduct; unless they are a "cornerstone of the organizational culture," they will not render the organization an ethical or responsible one.

So, in simple words, this aspired shift in practice requires a radical change in our mentality. Perhaps a more meaningful way to think about leadership is as a form of being (with ourselves and others); a way of thinking and acting that awakens and mobilizes people to find new, freer, and more meaningful ways of seeing, communicating, interacting, working, and living. And, it can be easily inferred that this is not a characteristic of people who are positioned high in the organizational or even political hierarchy. On the contrary, that kind of influence can show up when least expected. This form of leadership is anchored to personal self-awareness and mindfulness. Therefore, we devote the succeeding lines to discussing how notions that are predominantly within the purview of philosophy can be of benefit to the leadership relationship.

The Need for a Paradigm Shift

The majority of leadership books or academic papers start by directing our attention to the need for changing the leadership paradigm and usually end up with discussing that it is also imperative to change the way leadership is being taught in business schools. Most of the time they underpin their argument by using as an example the ethical scandals of Enron, WorldCom, or Tyco, or referring to major political ones, such as Watergate, Clinton–Lewinsky, or Berlusconi, among others. In other instances, the argument goes even deeper to suggest a leadership deficit, as exemplified by the recent events in Eurozone (see for example the fiscal crises in Greece, Ireland, Portugal, and Spain) and also in the more recent American financial collapse.

The bottom line for bringing up the above examples is to stimulate a discussion concerning, firstly, the morality of leaders as individuals and, secondly, the attribution of individual responsibility for these immoral actions.

Putting it differently, given that no causal relationship between a leader's personal history and unethical behavior has yet been established (and it is doubtful there ever will be…), we cannot safely infer that the leader *consciously* decided to act unethically. Obviously the key word here is consciously; if the leader was not *aware* that they were entering the darkness, we cannot blame them. But, we can teach them to become more aware and hence more capable of distinguishing between good and bad.

This last observation brings to the surface two important questions about the curriculum of modern business schools. Firstly, how many MBAs are taught that a "bottom line" based solely on finances is a tragic simplification? And secondly, how many MBAs prepare the leader to cope with high uncertainty, volatility, and emotional toxicity? In addition, as we become more aware that the world is chaotic and unpredictable, leaders face inevitable and unavoidable questions which their professional training did not prepare them:

- How do I plan when I don't know what will happen next?

- How do I maintain my values when worldly temptations abound?

- Do I have a purpose to my life?

- Where can I find meaning in my life?

- Where can I find the courage and faith to stay in course?

On top of that, leaders are expected to help other people, that is their followers, find meaning at work and navigate through various intra-personal, relational, and organizational problems and challenges. Furthermore, experience along with scientific evidence seems to converge that coercive and control leadership styles are doomed to fail, not only from an ethical point of view, but mainly because they are ineffective. The duty of leaders is not to create a safe and secure environment for their people or to give answers. Instead, they must provide the followers with the means to deal with uncertainty or educate them to search the answers for themselves. For example, a leader might see that teaching or showing their people a specific way of resolving a crisis is less useful than teaching their people a way to search for crisis solutions.

Undoubtedly, these ideas are not new; spiritual teachers have been doing this for millennia. But, the last generations have exhibited alienation and disregard of the spiritual dimensions of existence which has eventually led leaders to an existential threshold. We have forgotten that the real self is spiritual in its core; our being consists of fundamental beliefs, values, ultimate existential concerns and assumptions, and disregarding these may be the root cause of the existential crises (usually somatized as depression, anxiety, eating, or sexual disorders) that seem to emerge more often than ever before. Thus, if we are to succeed as good leaders in these difficult times, we should turn our attention inwards, start asking forgotten, repressed or unpleasant questions, and contemplate on our existence. Although the philosophical tradition of existentialism offers numerous distinctive and prominent quotes, the following words of director Stanley Kubrick grasps the essence of our thinking very well:

> *The very meaninglessness of life forces man to create his own meaning. Children, of course, begin life with an untarnished sense of wonder, a capacity to experience total joy at something as simple as the greenness of a leaf; but as they grow older, the awareness of death and decay begins to impinge on their consciousness and subtly erode their joie de vivre, their idealism—and their assumption of immortality. As a child matures, he sees death and pain everywhere about him, and begins to lose faith in the ultimate goodness of man. But, if he's reasonably strong—and lucky—he can emerge from this twilight of the soul into a rebirth of life's plan. Both because of and in spite of his awareness of the meaninglessness of life, he can forge a fresh sense of purpose and affirmation. He may not recapture the same pure sense of wonder he was born with, but he can shape something far more enduring and sustaining. The most terrifying fact about the universe is not that it is hostile but that it is indifferent; but if we can come to terms with this indifference and accept the challenges of life within the boundaries of death—however mutable man may be able to make them—our existence as a species can have genuine meaning and fulfillment. However vast the darkness, we must supply our own light.[6]*

A Philosophical Turn

There seems to be a change in opinion in leadership literature at the moment— welcomed and supported by a number of scholars including ourselves—as to which philosophy is of most use to leaders to enable them to handle the dual task they have been assigned; that is, to find a meaning in work life

---

6   Phillips, G.D. (2010). *Stanley Kubrick: Interviews*. Brighton, UK: Roundhouse Publishing Ltd, p. 73

(and potentially in life in general) and to help others to find it also. However, before we elaborate on this, let us clarify what we mean about philosophy, a discipline rather misunderstood these days. Starting from the etymology of the term, philosophy is a Greek word compound from the words philo (friend) and sophia (wisdom), mainly indicating the study of general and fundamental problems that concern human nature. According to Anthony Grayling,[7] "the aim of philosophical inquiry is to gain insight into fundamental questions about knowledge, truth, reason, reality, meaning, mind and value. Other human endeavors explore aspects of these same questions, not least art and literature, but it is philosophy that mounts a direct assault upon them". Philosophy is distinguished from other ways of addressing such problems by its critical, generally systematic approach and its reliance on rational argument. In more casual speech, by extension, "philosophy" can refer to "the most basic beliefs, concepts, and attitudes of an individual or group." Philosophy then is far from being an alienated and sterilized subject that only a specific group of people care about. On the contrary, if we really think about it, we all more or less engage in philosophical thinking at some point in our lives. Perhaps there is a trigger event (parenthood, accident, death) or just an unexpected and inexplicable moment that will initiate contemplation on the fundamentals of human life. Prince Hamlet, to give a literature example, asks himself "to be or not to be" after the death of his father. Although mystery and debate still surround the meaning of the phrase, it is more likely that Shakespeare puts these words in the mouth of his hero to express the fundamental question "why live"? And, although artists, poets, and writers have predominantly been concerned with these philosophical issues, the rest—depending on the according era and culture—have discovered ways or turned to an organized collection of beliefs, cultural systems, and world views that relate humanity to an order of existence in order to deal with them.

What differs nowadays and is worth talking about is that we have suppressed these thoughts so much that when these moments inevitably appear, we are taken by surprise. So, unprepared and without the necessary means to deal with them, they frequently leave us with exhausting, inconvenient, and hard to deal with depressive symptoms. These depressive symptoms have taken many names, but we frequently encounter them as existential crisis, angst, or anxiety, which according to James and Gilliland[8] is a moment at which an individual questions the foundations of his or her life; whether his or her life has any meaning, purpose, and value. It includes the inner conflicts

---

7   Graying, A.C. (2006). *Philosophy 1: A guide through the subject*. Retrieved 10 March 2013 from http://www.acgrayling.com/philosophy-1-a-guide-through-the-subject.
8   James, R.K., & Gilliland, B.E. (2013). *Crisis Intervention Strategies* (7th edn). Belmont, CA: Brooks/Cole.

and anxieties that accompany important human issues such as purpose, responsibility, independence, freedom, and commitment.

In the next few lines, we attempt to understand the origins of this situation; later on, we delve into the analysis of existential thinking as a meta-competence and its related concepts. We finish this chapter by suggesting that if philosophical thinking was not exiled from everyday and leadership practice, maybe it would add up to the transformation of our current amoral, indifferent, and unbalanced society into a more meaningful, purposeful, and ethical one.

The New God

All progress made by humankind in terms of theory, science, art, and civilization can be traced back to the contemplation of the origins and the future of the human race, that is, seeking to understand where one came from and what one's destination is. Putting it differently, in a continuous effort to make sense and add value to existence, establish self-worth and create a legacy, humanity has evolved arts, methods, and techniques to approximate an answer to the core existential questions (why am I here, what happens after death, what is life and so on). It is a fundamental human characteristic to look at the circumstances of one's life and ask, "Why?" No matter how poor or desperate we are, we always need to assign a reason to why things are as they are. Every known culture had its rituals and spiritual practices to deal with this fundamental quest. But today things are quite different since we increasingly move away from anything spiritual.

However, existential quest has not abandoned us yet and, given the alienation from our spiritual aspects at the expense of material ones, our chaotic and highly complex age has turned for answers to the contemporary god, namely, science. We've asked science to explain how to deal with chaos, catastrophes, and life's unpredictability. We want science to teach us how to prevent the sudden events that destroy lives and futures. We want science not just to explain chaos but to give us tools for controlling it. We expect from science to delay aging and maybe prevent dying and to get us out of all life's challenges. But, what we are asking is feasible only to a certain degree. Chaos can't be utterly controlled; the unpredictable can't be entirely predicted. Instead, we are being called to encounter life as it is: uncontrollable, unpredictable, messy, surprising, and erratic.

The philosophers of the nineteenth century warned that the reasons above would lead to existential crises. For example, Kierkegaard considered that angst and existential despair would appear when an inherited or borrowed world-view proved unable to explain unexpected and extreme life experiences. Nietzsche extended his views to suggest that the so-called Death of God, that is the loss of collective faith in religion and traditional morality, had created a more widespread existential crisis for the philosophically aware. Existential crisis has indeed been viewed as the inevitable accompaniment of modernism (1890 and beyond). The French philosopher Emile Durkheim saw individual crises as the by-product of social pathology and a partial lack of collective norms. From an existentialist point of view, existential crises are viewed as the result of the loss of meaning throughout the modern world. One can easily reckon that there are no easy remedies or prescriptions to deal effectively with existential problems. Perhaps the only notable exception is awareness. By being constantly aware and conscious of our existence, meaning is more likely to emerge.

So, What is Existential Thinking?

The first and simplest definition of the word existential is that it is related to existence. As follows, when we are engaged in existential thinking, we are thinking about our existence. All human beings, no matter the cultural background, ethnicity, age, educational level, or even era, have reflected on such matters as life and death, reality, consciousness, the universe, time, truth, justice, evil, and other similar issues. In the academic literature, such existential issues have been described as the "ultimate questions" of life. In fact, some authors have taken a step further, arguing that this kind of thinking can be conceptualized as capacity, ability, or even intelligence. For example, Nasel[9] described this capacity as "deliberation of existential issues and questions of ultimate concern (for example, death and afterlife), and inquiry into the meaning and origin of life" (p. 56). Accordingly, the well-known psychologist Howard Gardner argued that existential ability can be included in the theory of multiple intelligences,[10] given that some criteria are met (that is, cerebral identification and cognitive components). He described existential intelligence as "the intelligence of big questions" after having distinguished it from spiritual awareness, which is more a "state of being" rather than a computational set of skills. Existential intelligence is the ability to think about the big picture of life, understand life's mission and purpose, and craft meaning under adversity.

---

9   Nasel, D.D. (2004). Spiritual orientation in relation to spiritual intelligence: A new consideration of traditional Christianity and New Age/individualistic spirituality. Doctoral Dissertation, University of South Australia.
10 Gardner, H. (2000). A case against spiritual intelligence. *The International Journal for the Psychology of Religion*, 10(1), 27–34.

Another part of the literature regards existential thinking as a "quest for understanding answers" to these ultimate questions.[11] But in our opinion, in line with a number of researchers (see for example King),[12] is that such a "quest" or striving for answers represents behavior rather than ability. Specifically, the behavior of striving for answers to existential questions (which might involve, for example, reading literature on existential topics) would be better considered as an outcome, natural consequence, or correlate of this particular capacity.

To deepen our understanding of the concept even more, we should mention that there are a number of authors[13] who further define existential contemplation as involving meaning and purpose in life. It is quite difficult, indeed, to initiate any discussion on existential matters without wondering about the meaning and purpose of our existence. Nevertheless, in order to be scientifically accurate, we must keep in mind that thinking about one's existence and contemplating on meaning of life are two distinct mental processes that require different levels of contemplative and reflective depth. Besides, as shall be discussed later on, construction of meaning is more personalized and internal and is better related to other concepts such as emergence of values, beliefs, character, and so on. On the other hand, though, one might argue, and we could not but agree, that meaning and life purpose cannot be solid and authentic unless serious existential reflection has preceded.

Although existential thinking is more of a natural process and appears in everyone regardless of age (numerous studies have shown that kids often ask questions about life and death), the truth is that most of us do not start thinking about our place in the cosmos unless a trigger event has taken place in our lives (for example, birth of a child, death of a beloved one, value inconsistency, and so on). Until that moment, we carry on with our lives worrying and stressing about seemingly *important* things, and losing the connection with time. But, when that moment hits, we usually experience such feelings of anxiety or existential angst—as the existential philosophers tend to call it—that are nothing like those felt before, and thus no defense mechanism can be energized. To the best of our knowledge, modern societies (and we focus on them not because

---

11 Noble, E.P. (2000). The *DRD2* gene in psychiatric and neurological disorders and its phenotypes. *Pharmacogenomics*, 1(3), 309–333.

12 King, D.B. (2008). Rethinking claims of spiritual intelligence: A definition, model, and measure. *Unpublished Master's Thesis*, Trent University, Peterborough, ON.

13 Wolman, R.N. (2001). *Thinking with Your Soul: Spiritual intelligence and why it matters*. New York: Harmony Books and Zohar D., & Marshall, I. (2000). *SQ: Connecting with our spiritual intelligence*. New York: Bloomsbury Publishing.

the existential pressure is higher, but because previous societies were closer to nature and hence developed unique ways of dealing with existential questions) have omitted the inclusion of any formal training in the educational systems. Perhaps, the amoral economic system, the constant hedonistic hunt, and the pursuit of easiness do not leave room for the difficult and uncomfortable, but yet inherent to the human nature, questions to transcend the consciousness.

As follows, in the extremely demanding and competitive environment of modern enterprises, nobody dares to mention existential thinking or philosophy. Admittedly, this last word has nowadays some connotations that are far from desirable. Indeed, we have come to believe that philosophy lies at the opposite end of practice and is best left for philosophers. However, as already implied, the *profession* of philosophy did not always have the narrow and specialized meaning it does now. For instance, in ancient Greece it had the very opposite: instead of a specialized theoretical discipline, philosophy was a concrete way of life, a total vision of man and the cosmos in the light of which the individual's whole life was to be lived. In the exemplary *Republic*, Plato went even further to argue that only philosophers can be true leaders. Leadership refers not just to the exercise of power by individual persons in positions of authority; it also denotes those processes by which a subset of society sets the terms of social life for the community as a whole. The clarification is important because Plato does not talk about the excellences of individual leaders within his ideal regime: rather he talks about the general character of and social functions performed by what we will term leadership classes (namely the guardians and the philosophers). The philosophers represented reason. Each class in this society would be ruled, directly or indirectly, by reason. For the philosophers, this happens internally (via the rational part being in charge within their souls), and for the auxiliaries and money-makers, it happens by being governed by the philosopher–rulers.

In an ideal city perfectly constituted, no social class would have reason to envy any other. The money-making class would not envy the philosophers; after all the philosophers have no money, and do not spend their time enjoying material comforts and other sorts of things that motivate money-makers. Nor would the philosophers envy those who have more material goods than themselves; they would in fact not experience the lack as deprivation, since their souls would be ordered so as to desire first and foremost the pursuit of knowledge, with other types of pleasure playing a subordinate role.

The opportunity to include philosophy in the leadership relationship is not provided in traditional approaches despite the fact that it is philosophy that provides a framework within which we interpret our experiences and judge ourselves and situations.[14] It is true that a philosophical understanding can form the basis for understanding and thinking about leadership from a different perspective, and it can also form the basis for leading organizations differently. This is far deeper than thinking outside the box, but engaging with issues, such as the nature of social and organizational realities, thinking about the type of institutions we want to create and be a part of, and seeing the future as one of infinite possibilities.

A bright exception is the recent work of Cunliffe[15] who introduces the theme of philosopher leader, in which leadership becomes a process of thinking more critically and reflexively about ourselves, our actions, and the situations we find ourselves in. She notes, "All businessmen, whether or not we admit it, are philosophers in a sense. The philosopher leader thinks differently, asking: What is important? What if we think about organizations, leadership and ethics in this way rather than that? Where will it take us?"

However, as indicated in the beginning of the chapter, the current thinking on leadership has also begun to turn its focus to a rediscovery of the need to define, shape, and use the commonly held core values of the organization. For example, Fry defines spiritual leadership as "the values, attitudes and behaviors necessary to intrinsically motivate one's self and others so that they have a sense of spiritual survival through calling and membership."[16] Ethical leadership is another field in which one comes across notions of a more philosophical perspective, since the emphasis is put on the leader's moral character, the ethical legitimacy of the leader's vision, and the morality of the choices and actions that leaders engage in. The theory investigates both the antecedents and outcomes of ethical beliefs and perceptions.[17]

Also, the recent developments in authentic leadership have stressed the importance of authenticity, a philosophical matter by its very nature. Avolio et al.[18] define authentic leaders as "those who are deeply aware of their own

14 Rice, J.H. (1960). Existentialism for the businessman. *Harvard Business Review*, 38(2), 135–143.
15 Cunliffe, A.L. (2009). The philosopher leader: On relationalism, ethics and reflexivity—a critical perspective to teaching leadership. *Management Learning*, 40(1), 87–101.
16 Fry, L.W. (2003). Toward a theory of spiritual leadership. *The Leadership Quarterly*, 14(6), 693–727.
17 Brown, M.E., & Trevino, L.K. (2006). Ethical leadership: A review and future directions. *The Leadership Quarterly*, 17(6), 595–616.
18 Avolio, B.J., Gardner, W.L., Walumbwa, F.O., Luthans, F., & May, D.R. (2004). Unlocking the mask: A look at the process by which authentic leaders impact follower attitudes and behaviors. *Leadership Quarterly*, 15(6), 801–823.

and others' values/moral perspectives, knowledge, and strengths; aware of the context in which they operate; and who are confident, hopeful, optimistic, resilient and of high moral character." Authentic leaders are not only true to themselves, they are also true to their roles as leaders which also includes an element of being aware of social cues and followers' needs, expectations, desires, and feedback. Because the authentic leader is self-aware, he/she can react to environmental priming cues to make certain aspects of the true self more salient; authentic leaders ultimately sense their role more faithfully.

Evidently, in this leadership style, the role of self-awareness or personal insight of the leader is considered a key factor contributing to the development of authentic leadership. As originally defined, the self-awareness construct involves a cognitive state in which an individual focuses conscious attention on some aspects of the self. It says nothing about the degree of accuracy or inaccuracy of self-perceptions. According to several scholars, self-awareness arises by self-reflection about one's values, beliefs, attributes, and motives. Such self-reflection helps authentic leaders to know themselves and gain clarity and concordance with respect to their core values, identity, beliefs, emotions, motives, and goals. Authentic leadership thus begins with knowing yourself deeply. Hence, it can be argued that this self-reflection makes leaders more connected with their environment and therefore more believable.[19]

This more critical stance of viewing ourselves, and thereby others, inescapably leads to the realization that we are utterly responsible for the choices we make regarding the social interactions and institutions, the organizational life, or even the natural world. In this endeavor, a look at the philosophical oeuvres of Heidegger,[20] who devoted a great deal of attention to the importance of context in our understanding of ourselves as beings-in-the-world (*Dasein*), might be fruitful. He suggested that, "For the most part *Dasein* understands itself in terms of that which it encounters in the environment and that with which it is circumspectively concerned." However, he also suggested that our understanding of our environment is self-referential. In an attempt to decode this difficult idea, avoiding any over-simplification, we would say that *Dasein* is always somewhere; we are always in a place, doing things, and interacting with others and other things. We are all present in this world as beings that are united. Every one of our actions comes from the way we are conducting ourselves. And since *Dasein* comports itself toward being, so everything we do

---

19 Drucker, P. (1999). *Management Challenges of the 21st Century*. New York: HarperBusiness.
20 Heidegger, M. *(1962/1993) Being and Time. Reproduced in basic writings: Martin Heidegger* (edited by D. Farrell Krell). London: Routledge, p. 439.

comes from our way of existing in the world. So all social actors, and leaders for that matter, need to be responsible for how they act since everything around them affects them and signifies a world that has significance. Hence, for life to be meaningful, it has to have some kind of social significance.

If we wanted to find a correspondent idea in management studies, the central notion of vision would serve that purpose well as, according to Kotter, it "refers to a picture of the future with some implicit or explicit commentary on *why* people should strive to create that future.[21] At a hidden or more subjective level are values and beliefs, derived from how people justify and explain what they do.[22]

To sum up, successful leaders make the journey from seeing themselves as an independent entity to viewing themselves as part of a larger whole, and also help others toward this realization. We will now analyze the issues of meaning, self-awareness, mindfulness, and resilience, which derive from this existential meta-competence.

Meaningful Motivation

Our human needs for comprehensive perceptual frameworks and for a system of values on which to base our actions are the most important motivators as we search for meaning in life. When the meaning of life is lost (or not found), there are severe repercussions on our sense of well-being and our sense of wholeness. However, these breaks in our sense of wholeness are not the most severe of the repercussions, as loss of meaning can even lead to depression, detachment, disorientation, a sense of omnipotence, paranoia, psychosomatic complaints just to name a few. Many great minds, among them Wittgenstein, Kant, and Bruner, have attempted to answer the eternal question, "What does meaning making or making sense mean?" In the interest of brevity, let's just say that making sense is the process of arranging our understanding of experience so that we can know what has happened and what is happening, and do so that we can predict what will happen; it is constructing knowledge of ourselves and the world.

Drawing from the above definition, the link between this meaning-making process and leadership is not hard to establish. Leadership is a social phenomenon that people use to relate to each other, to make sense, to make meaning.

21 Kotter, J.P. (1996), *Leading Change*. Boston, MA: Harvard Business School Press, p. 68.
22 Schein, E. (1990), Organizational culture. *American Psychologist*, 45(2), 109–119.

Likewise, leadership in organizations can be seen under the prism of meaning making instead of influence and decision making. That being said, it is really surprising that the opportunity to discuss the intricacies of meaning in the leadership relationship has—more often than not—been missed in traditional objectivist approaches.

Recently, though, there have been several remarkable attempts to compensate for this gulf. For example, the role of leaders as "meaning makers" has been particularly appreciated as a major motivational factor and a sign of followers' psychological well-being in the recently developed theories of transformational, spiritual, charismatic, connective, and servant leadership. Accordingly, the issue of meaning is endemic to the conceptualization of the emerging authentic leadership development with twofold connotations ascribed to it. Firstly, meaning is related to self-awareness, as the latter refers to demonstrating an understanding of how one derives and makes meaning of the world and how that meaning making process impacts the way one views himself or herself over time. Secondly, meaning is anticipated to elicit positive work outcomes among followers through identification with a leader that displays high levels of transparency, integrity, and moral standards.[23]

In this work context, meaningfulness is defined as "the value of a work goal or purpose, judged to the individual's own ideals or standards."[24] Thus, meaning cannot be obtained simply by performing effectively, but mainly from feeling that one is in touch with and enacting goals that are expressions of who one believes she or he is. The issue of meaningful work has been researched in relation to organizational culture,[25] employee engagement,[26] and work alienation.[27] In the relevant literature, leaders are likely to have a meaningful effect on followers' well-being,[28] intrinsic motivation,[29] and positive

23 Avolio, B., & Gardner, W. (2005). Authentic leadership development: Getting to the root of positive forms of leadership. *The Leadership Quarterly*, 16(3), 315–338.

24 May, D.R., Gilson, R.L., & Harter, L.M. (2004). The psychological conditions of meaningfulness, safety and availability and the engagement of the human spirit at work. *Journal of Occupational and Organizational Psychology*, 77(1), 11–37.

25 Schein, E. (2004). *Organizational Culture and Leadership* (3rd edn). San Francisco, CA: Jossey-Bass.

26 Spreitzer, G.M. (1995). Psychological empowerment in the workplace: Dimensions, measurement and validation. *Academy of Management Journal*, 38(5), 1442–1465.

27 Souba, W.W. (2006). The inward journey of leadership. *Journal of Surgical Research* 131(2), 159–167.

28 Iles, P., & Preece, D. (2006). Developing leaders or developing leadership? The Academy of Chief Executives' Programmes in the North East of England, *Leadership*, 2(3), 317–340.

29 Deci, E.L., Connell, J.P., & Ryan, R.M. (1989). Self-determination in a work organization. *Journal of Applied Psychology*, 74(4), 580–590.

relationships.[30] These effects are rooted on the assumption that leadership is realized in "the process whereby one or more individuals succeed in attempting to frame and refine the reality of others",[31] by mobilizing and "managing meaning."[32]

However, there is an observation that needs to be made. This approach on meaning-making stands in sharp contradiction to the humanistic and existential literature which assumes that "the human being is, per definition and necessity, a being whose destiny is meaning, intentions and projects — thus, by nature, a person is involved in his or her being and in his or her becoming (to which alienation is an obstacle): a subject whose whole being is meaning and which has a need of meaning".[33] In other words, for meaning to be meaningful, it needs to be made individually rather than provided by those in positions of power.

At first glance the above argument may lead to nihilistic views of leaders' role concerning the creation of workplace meaning, as one could infer that true meaning is only a matter of ultimate subjectivity with the leader having nothing to contribute. However, a thorough examination, in conjunction with empirical findings and even historical events, reveals that meaning-making constitutes leadership through a socially-oriented sense of "what *is* and what is important".[34] In that sense, meaning-making designates culture, which happens through such processes as identifying vision and mission, framing problems, and setting goals signifying leadership as a phenomenon that structures and transforms reality.

Hence, leaders are considered responsible for providing meaning and purpose to members of a collectivity. Indeed, leaders who are able to provide some sort of direction to "why" questions are thought "to motivate others, reinforce collective ties, and direct collective action".[35] In support of this argument, the function of charisma has been found to provide an extensive

---

30 Peterson, S., & Luthans, F. (2003), The positive impact and development of hopeful leaders, *Leadership & Organization Development Journal*, 24(1), 26–31.
31 Smircich, L., & Morgan, G. (1982). Leadership: The management of meaning. *Journal of Applied Behavioural Science*, 18(2), 257–273.
32 Lips-Wiersma, M., & Morris, L. (2009). *Discriminating between meaningful work and the management of meaning. Journal of Business Ethics*, 88(3), 491–511.
33 Aktouf, O. (1992). Management and theories of organizations in the 1990s: Toward a critical radical humanism? *Academy of Management Review*, 17(3), 407–431.
34 Drath, W.H., & Palus, C.J. (1994). *Making common sense: Leadership as meaning-making in a community of practice*. Greensboro, NC: Center for Creative Leadership, p. 10.
35 Shamir, B., House, R.J., & Arthur, M.B. (1993). The motivational effects of charismatic leadership: A self-concept based theory. *Organization Science*, 4(4), 577–594.

and insightful explanation of how meaning develops followers' internalized commitment.[36]

Lastly, within the leadership context, the creation of personal meanings is likely to result in increased motivation to serve others. This might happen for at least two reasons. Firstly, there is evidence that suggests that leaders who have devoted time to self-exploration become more attentive and observant of the discrepancy between one's actions and relevant salient ideals.[37] In other words, people who are highly conscious of themselves are probably disturbed by the difference between what they are doing or planning to do at a point in time, on one hand, and what they believe they ought to be doing, on the other. Thus, if such individuals think they could help those in need and are conscious of this ideal, their self-awareness should motivate them to adhere to this salient ideal. And secondly, according to Duval & Wicklund, "self-awareness sustains the belief that one has significant personal responsibility for others."[38]

However, without a solid, philosophical foundation for their values, leaders cannot make a judgment on what is good for themselves or the organization,[39] rendering meaning difficult—if not impossible—to derive. Hence, it can be inferred that for meaning to be generated, a leader has to develop a reflective capacity in order to establish their perspective on the world. It comes naturally then to assume that the attribution of meaning presupposes existential thinking. This might mean that existential thinkers are triggered by the need to aid others toward a deeper exploration of their own sense of meaning. It might also mean that leaders who display high levels of existential thinking are expected to be more able to encourage or inspire followers to reflect upon their own sense of (life) purpose.

In a *Forbes* article, the above notions are perfectly illustrated through a comparison of two very popular American television shows, namely *The Apprentice* and *Undercover Boss*. In *The Apprentice*, the top managers are assigned to locate and fire the weakest links of a team. This task is realized by giving the team members simple jobs in order to expose their weaknesses. The winners of the show were those individuals who did not use the most ethical means to accomplish the

---

36 Conger, J.A., & Kanungo, R.N. (1988). The empowerment process: Integrating theory and practice. *Academy of Management Review*, 13(3), 471–482.
37 Duval, S., & Wicklund, R. (1972). *A Theory of Self-awareness*. New York: Academic Press.
38 Ibid.
39 Nonaka, I. and Toyama, R. (2007), Strategic management as distributed practical wisdom (Phronesis). *Industrial and Corporate Change*, 16(3), 371–394.

assigned tasks. All others were exiled. Their trophy was a job where they would maintain the cycle of power in addition to some exotic trips.

In the *Undercover Boss*, real-world CEOs, concealing their real identity, visit their own companies and learn first-hand from employees about their work, their goals, and what motivates them. In most cases, the executives come to realize that the people in their employment are enormously gifted and committed. Good employees find meaning in the day-to-day routines of their work. For example, an employee in a small supermarket knows the names of the customers to whom she sells coffee, thus nurturing relationships. Even a street cleaner finds meaning and pride in keeping an amusement park clean for guests. The moral of the story is that the employees who find meaning at work make a difference. That meaning may come from relationships, opportunities, the work environment, or the work itself.

Concluding, it is worth noting that at the end of *The Apprentice* there is one survivor while at the end of *Undercover Boss*, entire groups of employees stand and applaud their company, their colleagues, and their managers. In a nutshell, the leaders are responsible for providing to all employees at all levels of their organization compelling reasons to work, because when employees have a "why" to work toward, they can cope with any "what."

The Need for Mindfulness

For the leader to be able to see the whole picture, it is vital that she pays attention to the richness of her experiences and then attunes firstly with herself and later with the others. To put it another way, leaders need to be present and mindful. The value of being present cannot be overemphasized; we are continuously thinking about the past, we dream about the future, we worry, we anticipate, we fantasize about our lives, and thus we tend to forget about the present moment, which is actually what we really have.

The Buddhists have an expression to describe the phenomenon of the endless mind chatter. They call it the "monkey mind" paralleling our mind that jumps from thought to thought the same way as a monkey jumps from tree to tree. When we say, "Sorry, I had something else on my mind," that's monkey mind. As Eckhart Tolle put it in his landmark book, *The Power of Now*:

> *The mind is a superb instrument if used rightly. Used wrongly, however, it becomes very destructive. To put it more accurately, it is*

not so much that you use your mind wrongly—you usually don't use it at all. It uses you. This is the disease ... The instrument has taken you over.[40]

The antidote to monkey mind is mindfulness, a technique in which a person becomes intentionally aware of his or her thoughts and actions in the present moment, non-judgmentally. Being mindful is having a big picture awareness that gives us a measure of objectivity about what we are thinking. It helps us step outside habituated responses and solve problems more creatively.

In this book, we have several times stressed the need for a new way of being—in our selves, in our institutions, and in our relationships. Our modern culture has evolved in recent times to create a troubled world with individuals suffering from alienation, schools failing to inspire and to connect with children, a modern society without a moral compass helping clarify how we can move forward in our global community. A light at the end of the tunnel might be the cultivation of an experiential understanding of the mind. Through mindful awareness, we can learn to embrace our own inner world and the mind of others with kindness and compassion.

When we are fully present in the moment and we quiet our dominating monkey mind (which takes practice and discipline), we make room to experience our lives through the remaining aspects of the Self that is—heart, body, and spirit. Presence opens the way to directly experiencing our deep connection to the rest of the world. The more we experience "unity" or "oneness," the less of an abstract idea it becomes. The goal is not to experience some fantasized version of unity that is naturally harmonious, instead it is to fully grasp how interconnected everything is, which helps us bring into focus that the consequences of all of our actions, big and small, impact others and the planet.

Through the practices of presence and mindfulness we begin to see how the *process* of our own activism for seeking change matters. If we are using a peaceful process we are creating more peace. As we become more aware of the impact that our own actions have on others, we can become more committed to the whole and be motivated to shift our activism approach away from the dominant adversarial "us versus them" framework toward a unifying "we're all in the same boat" framework.

---

40 Tolle, E. (2004). *The Power of Now: A guide to spiritual enlightenment*. Vancouver, BC: Namaste Pub.

Mindfulness and Leadership: An Attainable Link

In organizational science, mindfulness is a relatively new concept, but recently scholars have shown an increased interest in its significance in organizational processes. Particularly in the field of leadership, mindfulness serves as a process that counters the unprecedented challenges that leaders face nowadays.[41] Although mindfulness in Eastern thought has its origins in Buddhist traditions, Langer's recent description of mindfulness is representative of Western thinking and has been adopted by several organizational researchers. The author defined mindfulness as "a state of alertness and lively awareness that is manifest in active information processing, characterized by the creation and refinement of categories and distinctions and the awareness of multiple perspectives." In Langer's model,[42] the rich awareness associated with a mindful state of being is expressed at the individual level in at least three ways: active differentiation and refinement of existing categories and distinctions; creation of new discontinuous categories out of the continuous streams of events that flow through activities; and a more nuanced appreciation of context and alternative ways to deal with it. By remaining alert to potential changes in their situation, mindful individuals are more adaptive and responsible to shifts in their environments. This fosters a rich action repertoire with which to successfully address the unknown; it also generates energy, clearheadness, and joy.

Although mindfulness has been conceptualized as distinct to self-awareness, insofar as it involves receptive attention to internal psychological states, it is found to be associated with self-attunement, understanding, and clarity of thoughts and emotions.[43] Mindfulness is likely to facilitate conditions of open awareness that can be especially valuable for choosing behaviors that are consistent with one needs, values, and interests. It can be argued, then, that the absence of mindfulness in an individual would be associated with lower levels of self-awareness. Recently, Hede[44] introduced a new model that incorporates two types of mindfulness which can be used by managers to increase self-awareness, their capacity to handle emotional reactivity, and reduce stress. In the same way, Boyatzis and McKee[45] view mindfulness as an

41 Boyatzis, R., & McKee, A. (2005), *Resonant Leadership: Sustaining yourself and connecting with others through mindfulness, hope, and compassion*. Boston, MA: Harvard Business School Press.
42 Langer, E. (1989).*Mindfulness*. Reading, MA: Addison-Wesley.
43 Ryan, R.M., & Brown, K.W. (2003). Why we don't need self-esteem: On fundamental needs, contingent love, and mindfulness. *Psychological Inquiry*, 14(1), 27–82.
44 Hede, A. (2010). The dynamics of mindfulness in managing emotions and stress. *Journal of Management Development*, 29(1), 94–110.
45 Boyatzis, R.E., & McKee, A. (2005). *Resonant Leadership: Renewing yourself and connecting with others through mindfulness, hope, and compassion*. Boston: Harvard Business School Press.

essential element of resonant leadership and define it as the capacity to be fully aware of what is happening inside and around us. Similarly, Carroll[46] suggests that a mindful leader demonstrates an inner authenticity that manifests itself through elegance, command, gentleness, and intelligence.

Ultimately, it has been stated that mindfulness cannot be fully captured with words because it is a subtle, non-verbal experience.[47] It is a way of relating to all experience, be it positive, negative, or neutral, such that our overall level of suffering is reduced and our sense of well-being increases.[48] To be mindful is to be alert, to be able to recognize what is happening at each present moment. Thus, we suggest that mindfulness can be considered as a vehicle for a leader to see beyond the constraints of the everyday routine and eventually become aware of the meaning she or he ascribes to life. Presence and mindfulness also helps us clear away our defensiveness, negative assumptions, and habitual ways of seeing and hearing things, opening new paths for dealing with conflicting points of view. This function of mindfulness, that is breaking the habitual patters of thinking, is directly linked to another competence that the modern leader needs to cultivate—resilience. In the following chapter we will discuss the meaning of resilience, its importance in everyday leadership practices, and its relation to mindfulness and existential thinking.

Resilience

Resilience is defined as "the developable capacity to rebound or bounce back from adversity, conflict and failure, or even positive events, progress, and increased responsibility."[49] Resilience allows not only reactive recovery but also proactive learning and growth through the challenges we face. The capacity for resilience promotes the recognition and acknowledgement of the impact of both negative and positive overwhelming events, allowing the affected individual the time, energy, and resource investment to recover, rebound, and return to an equilibrium state. Thus, resilience places a unique positive value on risk factors that may otherwise be viewed as threats that increase the probability of negative outcomes or decrease the probability of positive ones. Living resiliently is more

---

46 Carroll, M. (2007). *The Mindful Leader: Ten principles for bringing out the best in ourselves and others*. Boston, MA: Trumpeter.

47 Gunaratana, H. (1994). *Mindfulness in Plain English*. Boston, MA: Wisdom Publications.

48 Kabat-Zinn, J. (2005). *Coming to Our Senses: Healing ourselves and the world through mindfulness*. New York: Hyperion.

49 Luthans, F. (2002). Positive organizational behavior. Developing and managing psychological strengths. *Academy of Management Executive*, 16(1), 57–72.

than just "bouncing back." It is about shifting our perceptions, changing our responses, and learning something new. For example, a resilient response to losing your job might re-contextualize and reframe the situation in any of the following ways:

- "I'm sure that there's a lesson or two for me to learn from all this."

- "It would be easy to get 'just another job'. I'm going to find one that I'm truly passionate about."

Living resiliently represents a whole new way of being and doing. In this way, resilience isn't just for the hard times, it's for all times. Empowering us to live, love, and work adventurously in the face of change, it builds a well from which we can draw for the rest of our lives. Resilient people devise conceptions about their suffering to create some sort of meaning for themselves and others. This dynamic of meaning making is, most researchers agree, the way resilient people build bridges from present day hardships to a fuller, better constructed future. Those bridges make the present "manageable" (for a lack of a better term) removing the sense that the present is overwhelming. As a result, resilient people experience "increased self-reliance and self-efficacy; heightened awareness of one's vulnerability and mortality; improvement in ties to others— greater self-disclosure and emotional expressiveness, more compassion and capacity to give to others; clearer philosophy of life".[50] In the same vein, we can argue that resilient qualities result in introspection, adaptation, growth, self-understanding, and wholeness.

As such, resilience is related to mindfulness, and not just conceptually but also biologically. Indeed, there is evidence supporting that practicing mindfulness exercises can lead to faster recovery from emotional arouses. The neuroscientist Richard Davidson[51] has conducted a series of tests from which he concluded that there is a link between mindfulness and arousal of a particular part of the brain, called the amygdala. The amygdala is involved in the processing of emotions such as fear, anger, and pleasure. It is also responsible for determining what memories are stored and where the memories are stored in the brain. It is thought that this determination is based on how huge an emotional response an event invokes. According to Davidson,

---

50 Ryff C., & Singer, B. (2003). Flourishing under fire: Resilience as a prototype of challenged thriving, in C. Keyes & J. Haidt (Eds), *Flourishing: Positive psychology and tile life well-lived* (pp. 15–36). Washington, DC: American Psychological Association.

51 Davidson, R.J. (2010). Empirical explorations of mindfulness: Conceptual and methodological conundrums. *Emotion*, 10(1), 8–11.

practicing mindfulness affects the rapidity with which the amygdala recovers after an emotional arousal (let's just say from a stressful situation). And what's more there seems to exist a correlation between the number of hours of formal meditative practice and the rapidity with which the amygdala recovers. Then, the more mindful we become, the more we broaden and build several inner resources that help us strengthen our resilience.

At the organizational level, or specifically to leadership development, resiliency has been acknowledged as an important skill, as is evident from the interest from corporations, educational institutions, and the media, but there is still room to grow. In a television talk program, Arianna Huffington underlined that at the World Economic Forum in Davos, held in January 2013, the sessions on mindfulness and meditation were full and oversold.

What's causing this dramatic shift in our consciousness about what it takes today to be an effective leader? It starts with the changes taking place in the world. We live in an era of globalization and rapid technological change that is creating volatility, uncertainty, chaos, and ambiguity (VUCA is the acronym created by the US Military Academy to describe the world of the twenty-first century). Its impact is compounded by the rapidly changing job market and the new 24/7 communications world. This creates stress for executives and the institutions they lead. For institutions, the velocity of the business cycle and risks of the multi-polar global environment create instability. For individuals, the volatility creates more emotional ups and downs and can cause us to lose confidence. Amid such volatility, a reserve of mental and physical energy is required to be resilient. In his book, *Seven Lessons for Leading in Crisis*, Bill George[52] argues that resilience is the combination of heartiness, toughness, and buoyancy of spirit. These qualities are necessary for leaders to persevere through struggling moments, bounce back from adversity, and adapt to external stress.

The focus of resilience also goes beyond just the sum total of one's assets and risk factors. It incorporates the adaptational processes and mechanisms that combine assets and risk factors in a cumulative, interactive pattern. Resilience albeit germane is something different from hope or optimism as the latter apply more to situations that can be approached with a plan and can be reasonably explained through identifiable causes. In contrast, resilience recognizes the need for flexibility, adaptation, even improvisation, in situations predominantly characterized by change and uncertainty. It goes beyond the successes and failures associated with the current situation. Resilience is the capacity to search for and

---

52 George, B. (2009). *Seven Lessons for Leading in Crisis*. San Francisco, CA: Jossey-Bass.

find meaning despite circumstances that do not lend themselves to planning, preparation, rationalization, or logical interpretation. It develops in the face of adversity when leaders can elevate themselves over their difficult present, and values play a salient role in presenting different approaches for interpreting and shaping events. Most importantly, the role of values in enhancing leader's resiliency is largely based on the stability of those values as a source of meaning.

Concluding Thoughts

There are so many forces that lie beyond our control, but yet we are responsible for our own decisions and actions, as well as our own future, or the future of our organization or even community, because of free will and human agency. But before anything else, for that responsibility to be realized, we need to turn our attention inwards. The direction of our efforts should be focused in order to answer some of the major existential questions. If we wanted to make a list of the questions that classically and universally preoccupy the mind of human beings, regardless of age, race, education, or level of urbanization, we would end up with the following:

- Who am I?

- What should I do with my life?

- Where do I belong?

- What will happen to me after I die?

- What would make my life more meaningful and significant?

- What kind of world do we want?

- What does this mean for the kinds of societies we want?

- What is the role of business and economy?

- What should business contribute to such a new world?

- What kind of leaders do we need to achieve such a transformation?

- And as a result what kind of management education do we need?

We have argued earlier that engaging in existential thinking ends up with producing more questions than the initial trigger event or thought. There are three types of responses to existential quest; the first one is that we adopt an apathetic and indifferent stance and thus we do not engage in any type of searching. This is consistent with Frankl's[53] basic contention that a new type of neurosis (*noogenic neurosis*) is increasingly seen in clinics today and supposedly constitutes about 55 percent of the typical present-day load. This neurosis arises largely as a response to a complete feeling of emptiness of purpose in life. The chief dynamic is "existential frustration" created by a sense of vacuum of perceived meaning in personal existence, and manifest in the symptom of boredom. According to Frankl, the essence of human motivation is the "will *to* meaning" (*Der Wille zum Sinn*); when meaning is not found, the individual becomes "existentially frustrated."[54] The second type of response is that we postpone the quest, either because we have the answer that best serves our current condition and lifestyle or because we think that we cannot deal with the potential unpleasant sentiments that the quest might incite (for example, realization that our job does not satisfy our real needs or that we do not like the social cycles we have created or our marriage is not fulfilling).

Finally, we can actively engage in different stages of the meaning quest, thus restoring a healthy sense of the self. From that point of view, existential thinking enables us to fathom our self and our role in the world. That is synonymous with reconciling the negative and positive aspects of the self and avoiding illusions and delusions of the self. In that sense, self-concept is an ongoing process of meaning-making and meaning-reconstruction. But, a solid self-concept requires the essential process of self-reflection on our experiences. Through this process, which is lasting and constant, we are able to go beyond the mechanical and institutional levels of existence and discover what really is important.

Certainly, leaders today are faced with enormous challenges, most of them not of their own doing. As times grow more chaotic, as people question the meaning (and meaninglessness) of this life, people start looking for leaders to save and rescue them. Historically, people have often given away their freedom and allowed dictatorship when confronted with uncertainty. And of course there have been individuals who took advantage of the contingencies, and in their effort to make things better or out of personal ambitions,

---

53 Frankl, V. (1969). *The Will to Meaning; Foundations and applications of logotherapy.* New York: World Pub. Co.
54 Ibid.

they exerted more control over the disorder. What's more, they tried to give answers to dilemmas that have no answers. No leader can achieve this on behalf of someone else. So, is there anything the leader can do to help? Perhaps cultivating existential thinking.

Consequently, existential thinking serves at least two important functions; on one hand, it can help people manage their own personal adversities and maybe discover their true calling and purpose and, on the other hand, enable them as leaders to help others cope with difficult situations, show their best self and sustain high levels of performance. In this work, we make the case for thinking about leadership as a way of being that is reflective and thoughtful about self, others, and the world we live in; that values relationships and the present moment; that is connected to others and embodied; that is not narrowly striving or ego-driven; and that is liberating in its effects. Moreover, self-reflection helps leaders to cope with the predicaments and paradoxes they face on a daily basis, for in time this process develops a healthy and open sense of the self and clarifies one's place in this world.

Therefore, taking into consideration all the capacities, inclinations, goals, values, cognitive powers, traits, and temperamental dispositions of an existentially intelligent person, we can assume that the profile of a leader that actively engages in existential thinking seems to meet the modern organizations' needs and expectations very well. Moreover, the deriving competencies, namely authenticity, meaning-making, mindfulness, and resilience can, on one hand, help leaders quell the everyday inner conflicts, maintain self-control, and deal with the inevitable crises and, on the other hand, assist others to do the same. To put it another way, this type of leaders may serve as change agents, transforming their capacity to lead into a "contagious affair"; their authentic stance of life and their intensive quest for meaning may motivate their surroundings toward mindful and resilient approaches in a continuously changing social context.

Chapter 3
Phronesis

Introduction

THE WORLD WE LIVE IN

We live in a time in which globalization and technological advancements have brought people and businesses closer than ever before. Moreover, open markets offer a huge potential for rapid and valuable communication and dissemination of knowledge throughout the planet. This new era of the so-called "global network economy" has laid the foundations for growth and development for individuals, businesses, and nations.

However, inevitably, this shift from the industrial to a new "knowledge era" has also caused several important problems that need to be addressed. High on that list of the problems that we need to think about is the role that leadership plays in both business and political systems. The bygone decades, deeply affected by the free market dogma (as epitomized by Milton Friedman), have left us with the idea that the sole purpose of business is to use its resources in order to maximize its profits and that we can render leadership responsible for keeping up those performance indicators. As logically follows, the unilateral orientation to results has produced a plethora of immoral and amoral leadership examples (Enron would be the highlight, business-wise) and an abundance of unhappy and depressed individuals (both leaders and employees). On top of that, modern leadership has to deal with a series of rather unpredictable economic and political circumstances (such as, for example, the global financial crisis, the impact of which has lasted much longer than originally anticipated), which are forcing major changes in the organization of modern business and in the goals that managers and leaders are meant to serve.

A second major issue that troubles contemporary thinkers concerns the apathy toward and alienation from the political happenings, both from the point of citizens and from organizations. This indifferent attitude toward politics is rather remarkable given that, throughout history, people were primarily interested (if not involved) in political affairs. Although the analysis of the reasons interpreting this stance extends beyond the limits of this book, we should just mention that there seems to be a lack of trust in elected politicians to serve the common good and a view that they are driven by other, personal (for example, hunger for power) or economic interests. Additionally, it is believed that there is a growing inconsistency between what is promised and fulfilled and also that individual agency (as exemplified by the action of voting) does not produce any change since the political status quo is determined by other stronger forces (mainly economic). What's more, the complex and detached political language, the myriad of corruptive political leaders, and the glorification of consumption has created this vicious cycle of moral debt, poverty, psychological deprivation, and so on.

These conditions emphatically highlight the need to revise the basic principles and practices of modern management in this increasingly complex and challenging business environment. First and foremost, top executives need to depart from the traditional performance-oriented approaches and integrate a more holistic attitude in their organizations. This holistic approach acknowledges that people (both employees and leaders) bring to work the whole spectrum of their self (that is, spiritual, psychological, social, and physical) and that maintaining a good life, maximizing well-being, or serving a meaningful purpose might occupy the first places—or at least before any career advancements or paycheck increases—in a list of the reasons that motivates them to work hard.

Secondly, in order to break the pattern of amorality, alienation, and corruption and replace it by a more desirable virtuous cycle, we need to pause and reflect on the fundamental values (such as honesty, fairness, dignity, and honor), learn from experience, history, and nature and, as follows, transform our educational paradigms accordingly. Now, this is easier said than done; it also takes time to change the well-established results-oriented and individualized mentality, but above all it takes will and courage as all radical changes demand. In this mission, a good starting point would be the return to philosophy— as Dov Seidman aptly puts it in a *Business Week* article, philosophy may be the "killer app" that will help us address those existential challenges that the world currently confronts and are briefly described above. As already mentioned in Chapter 2, philosophy explores the deepest, broadest questions of life— why we exist, how society should organize itself, how institutions should relate to society, and the purpose of human endeavor, to name just a few.

Indeed, philosophical approach seems to be more relevant than ever in light of the crises that our organizations and countries face. There is a need to create a new framework for understanding the world, addressing how we as humans seek alignment in our relationships and among competing interests. Specialized expertise is simply not enough to overcome the plethora of crises that the planet deals with nowadays (see for example, credit, climate, consumption, poverty, diseases and so on). These problems, like most issues businesses confront in the global marketplace, feature complex interdependencies that require an understanding of how political, financial, environmental, ethical, and social factors influence each other. The most appropriate discipline to connect the dots is philosophy—linking competing interests requires philosophers to examine areas that modern-day domain experts too often ignore: core beliefs, ethics, and character. So, when we say we need to return to a philosophical approach in relation to problem solving and management, we do not mean that practical aspects are getting out of the equation but rather that we need to broaden our understanding of problems by taking a deeper look at our own beliefs, values, ethics, and character, and comprehension of how they relate to those of others who share a stake in our problem-solving efforts. In other words, what we primarily need is to ask the right questions; and asking the right questions sometimes means that we need to open our eyes and see the big picture. This has grown more difficult in the modern organizational context as more businesses focus on specialized markets and hire specialized experts.

To give an example of how adapting philosophical attitude affects the behavioral aspects of businesses, the first issue that we need to keep in mind is that, just like philosophers, we as individuals and organizations need to keep values, ethics, and the overall human condition in mind whenever we make decisions and engage in actions. This means that we start by hiring for character (and not only for specialized skills), we continue by considering the long-term implications (in addition to the short-term rewards) of our decisions, and we finally look for ways to create value (in addition to extracting value). By taking these steps and embracing a more philosophical approach toward the *raison d'être*, structure, decision making, and problem solving, we prepare the ground for transforming businesses into more meaningful and worthwhile institutions.

In the ensuing chapters, drawing from the Eastern and Western ethical philosophical tradition, we will initiate a discussion about how ethics can be an integral and inseparable part of business organizations. Special attention is given to the notion of phronesis, both from the ancient and the contemporary analyses, since it is a concept that best describes the equilibrium that leaders of modern organizations need to find in order to be profitable and socially considerate. The reader should keep in mind, though, that this endeavor might generate more questions than answers, but we believe that actively searching and challenging the existing thinking patterns and questing for non-given or unfamiliar ways to approach problems and situations inevitably leads to the emergence of the most desirable business attributes, namely creativity and innovation. Besides, is it not the case that the most original and imaginative people are artists—traditionally considered to be individuals who have high philosophical and existential concerns?

Ethics

Ethics has always been the center of philosophical contemplation, as is evident in numerous ancient scripts (from Sanskrit epics of ancient India to Confucian Analects and the Homeric works) and modern writings (selectively Nietzsche, Kant, and Schopenhauer). However, philosophical ethics, as opposed to other areas such as ontology, have also been applied to real life. Aristotle, for example, believed that there was no point in studying ethics unless it would have some beneficial effect on the way one lived one's life. In the twentieth century, there has been a renewed interest in ethics as is evident in particular issues of contemporary practical concern (see, for example, meta-ethics or medical ethics, bioethics, and so on).

This development is part of a wider movement involving research into the ethical requirements on those with particular occupations. Some of this research is related to scientific advances and its implications for public policy. In the particular context we are discussing in this book, the last decades have given rise to the idea of business ethics, which deals with abstract issues concerning the nature, roles, and obligations of corporations but also with more concrete issues in the workplace, such as confidentiality or whistle-blowing. In this line of research there has been sufficient evidence suggesting that people tend to behave less ethically when they are part of organizations or groups. Additionally, individuals who may do the right thing in normal situations seem to adopt surprisingly different behaviors when operate under stressful conditions. And by individuals, we mean both leaders and followers. It should be noted though that the normal problems that need to be dealt with are mostly everyday work practices as opposed to large-scale ethical situations. But there lies the essence of initiating a discussion on business ethics; if we are able to develop practical ethical awareness in these everyday practices, then major ethical dilemmas will probably fall short.

The question that naturally surfaces here is why we do not use the accumulated knowledge about ethics and leadership alike in order to avoid the emergence of ethical controversies or, when emerged, deal with them appropriately. The answer to that is manifold. A first approach is that often there is an inconsistency between what the top management preaches and what frontline people understand and do. Secondly, there are a great many leaders who do not use this knowledge appropriately and an even greater number who do not cultivate the right types (for example, there is a tendency to place more importance on explicit knowledge when confronted with changing conditions). Furthermore, ethics and all the derivative parameters, such as social responsibility and morality, are not the primal focus of management education and hence are rarely incorporated into a MBA curriculum.

However, when taking a closer look at companies, we are encountering a paradox. Indeed, it is quite difficult to pinpoint a company (and a nation if we want to take it even further) that does not proclaim a high level of ethical standards in their structuring and functioning. Following the trend of the past decades, companies, especially larger ones, probably pay considerable attention to establishing long and detailed lists of ethical codes concerning the treatment of customers or environmental resources, special social groups (special needs, the unemployed, and so on), or all of the above. Now, if all the rules on those lists were genuinely followed we would hardly and rarely encounter any conduct mischief, environmental mismanagement, or ethical scandals. But apparently this is not the case (Enron, for example, had an extensive ethical code), a fact that can safely lead us to the argument that ethical codes are mainly used for their symbolic value in satisfying stakeholders and improving the corporate image. Elaborating on this argument, we can fairly presume that if no one is watching, there is a good chance that the corporations do not implement these codes, which renders profit (not ethics) the purpose of having codes in the first place.

To add another perspective to the above discussion, we can think about whether adherence to ethical codes or rules might reduce ethical awareness. To paraphrase, is it maybe that the mere and simple following of ethical codes can make people believe that they are acting ethically? It seems that this holds true for individuals and organizations given that ethical codes are primarily composed with the company's interests in mind rather than providing guidance for acting ethically. Unthinking and mechanical following of the rules is likely to remove the sense of personal responsibility from the agent, especially when they find themselves in legal gray areas or in an ambiguous situation that has not been foreseen by the ethical code (see, for example, matters concerning technology). But, on the other hand, this should not prevent us from expecting companies to have an ethical code for two main reasons: firstly, ethical codes or rules cannot deal with the ethical complexity and ambiguity of many situations.

Therefore, there is absolutely no certainty in assuming that what seemed just or appropriate in one situation will work the same in another. Secondly, we cannot and should not presume that sticking to formal ethical codes automatically signifies an ethical individual or organization. Actually, the fact of compliance with ethical rules and being ethical is rather contradictory, since an ethical person does not need rules to act ethically. Thus, in line with Aristotle, who will be given special attention in this chapter, we argue that actions need to be voluntary to be ethical.

The problems surrounding ethical and legal issues have ancient roots, and seemingly are still timely. As can be inferred from the aforementioned argument, one cannot equate ethics (systems of rules of conduct, socially sourced) and morality (inherent principles or habits, individual sourced). So, if we wanted to recapitulate, a person/organization following ethical principles may not have any morals. Likewise, one could violate ethical principles within a given system of rules in order to maintain moral integrity. On the other hand, a moral person may *choose* to follow a code of ethics as it would apply to a system of values.

Acknowledging the risk of delving into the deep waters of moral philosophy, we still need to understand what distinguishes a person who needs codes to act ethically from the one that is internally ethical. Although the answer is far from simple or one-dimensional, it seems to be that virtues, which are the main components of character, can provide valuable explanations. Virtues are attitudes, dispositions, or character traits that enable us to be and to act in ways that allow us to pursue our human potential for moral excellence. They permeate our state of being and dispose us to action. Virtues develop through learning and practice. The road to becoming virtuous requires a person to be constantly motivated by moral goods in their actions, meaning that if honesty, for example, is rarely associated with desired outcomes, then the agent might not choose to pursue it. Repetition of virtuous actions can lead to an individual acquiring good habits.

However, virtues are not just habits. They are habits in that once acquired they become characteristic of a person, but for an act to be considered virtuous, it requires choice, understanding, and knowledge. The virtuous agent has come to recognize the value of virtue and view it as the appropriate response in a given situation. The more virtuous the agent is, the more clearly a virtuous act will be judged as a good thing to do. This is a result of the intimate link between human intelligence and will, which brings us to the concept of phronesis. Phronesis, translated mostly as practical wisdom or prudence, reflects the capacity to make wise decisions regarding which virtues are the most appropriate in particular situations and the best way to enact those virtues.

Furthermore, Arjoon[1] asserts that phronesis assists not only with judging well, but also in carrying out the judgment made; he calls phronesis "a disposition to act." He explains this as follows:

> *Philosophers have long realized the gap between knowledge (to know the good) and action (to do the good). It is precisely the virtues, in particular phronesis, that establish the link between knowing and doing; virtues regulate the dynamic interplay between knowledge and behavior in concrete situations.*

In the past years, there have been numerous attempts to transfer the concept of phronesis to the business context, with the most representative and extensive work being that of Nonaka and Toyama,[2] which we will refer to later on. However, other important researchers have also recognized the importance of phronesis for modern organizations. So, for example, Bragues[3] writes about how practical wisdom has "the task of guiding action through the thickets of particularity. It overcomes the vagueness inherent in merely knowing that morally virtuous conduct is a mean between two extremes; it assists in pinpointing that mean in the situation at hand, taking into account all the relevant details and contingencies."

Now, if the leader wants organizational members to act ethically, they need to be able to take ethical decisions and to be given scope to reflect upon decisions. Giving people time to reflect upon and discuss their activities does not necessarily change them but it does make change more likely. The alternative is to enforce disciplinary and controlling pressures to make people behave in certain ways. But, rules or principles will not get us there, since we cannot expect people to act ethically if they are not given an opportunity to exercise practical ethical judgment. Too many codes or rules or control may lead to the exact opposite outcome, since there will always be situations that the ethical codes cannot cover and the good action cannot be planned beforehand.

To summarize, all social phenomena, including business, are context dependent and there is no point in trying to figure out what is good or just or whatever else in each situation unless we take into consideration the goals, values, and interests of the people involved. The role of leadership then becomes

1   Arjoon, S. (2007). Reconciling situational social psychology with virtue ethics. *International Journal of Management Review*, 10(3), 221–243.
2   Nonaka, I. and Toyama, R. (2007). Strategic management as distributed practical wisdom (Phronesis). *Industrial and Corporate Change*, 16(3), 371–394.
3   Bragues, G. (2006). Seek the good life, not money: The Aristotelian approach to business ethics. *Journal of Business Ethics*, 67(4), 341–357.

more thoughtful of society's interest; without undermining the importance of their organizational sustainability, leaders need to ask if the decisions are also good for society, for the greater good. In that way, companies will then realize that they are a part of the whole and their mission is to create lasting benefits for society. As the Greek philosopher Heraclitus so elegantly put it almost 2,500 years ago: "Character is fate," meaning that who we are as individuals determines what kind of life we will live and the experiences we will have.

Values from Ancient Eastern and Western Philosophy

Before moving to the analysis of the core concepts of this chapter, we feel that we need to open a parenthesis and justify ourselves against a potential critique of being nostalgic of past concepts and ideas. In our defense, one of the major roles of scientific inquiry concerns the need for finding values and ideas for companies and their executives which can be considered universal and eternal. Although each generation is responsible for developing their own values, and there should be trust that we are getting what we need, it seems that there have been some drawbacks. Indeed, the evolution of our economic situation (mainly referring to capitalism) has made us forget the essential nature of humanity—estranging us from nature and preventing us from realizing the interconnectedness between, and among, people and the universe. Therefore, it might be helpful to go back in time, studying and poring over the values and ideas that shaped the monumental ancient civilizations. Those values are pervasive in the teachings of the ancient Greek, Chinese and Indian philosophers that have influenced and shaped the thinking and action in both East and West. In this chapter we particularly focus on the concept of phronesis, as proposed by Aristotle and the Chinese philosophers, but we also take the idea further by establishing the connection with the modern business environment. Aristotle was the first philosopher to introduce the concept of phronesis as a master virtue of human nature. In his time, phronesis was deemed an important personal virtue, whilst in recent years, for many theorists of management phronesis (or practical wisdom as it is alternatively encountered), it is considered to play an important role in effective leadership. Specifically, phronesis offers leaders the opportunity to learn through experience, intuition, and vision.

Defining the Aristotelian Phronesis

Phronesis, then, originated by Aristotle, is defined as the habit of making the right decisions and taking the right actions in context, and the relentless pursuit of excellence for the common good. It reflects a learned ability to make judgments in accordance with the development of virtue, and with experience gained over time. Aristotle describes phronesis in *Nicomachean Ethics* as a virtue with two components; an intellectual and a moral one. The intellectual component is responsible for rendering the individual able to distinguish the good from the bad while the moral component forces him to act by employing the right means. The philosopher argues that it is impossible for someone to be characterized as good unless she or he is wise, moral, and virtuous. Aristotle holds that a person's good character not only influences their actions but also their perception. In his own words:

> The wise do not see things in the same way with those who look for personal advantage. The practically wise are those who understand what is truly worthwhile, truly important, and thereby truly advantageous in life; who know, in short, that is worthwhile to be virtuous.

Aristotle defined phronesis as part of a triad concept comprised of scientific knowledge and technical knowledge. Aristotle makes a distinction between phronesis and episteme (επιστήμη), which translated means scientific knowledge, and which concerns universals and knowledge tested in time and space. Then, he contrasts phronesis with techne (τέχνη), which translated means technical knowledge or craft knowledge, and which is context-dependent and related to the most effective way to reach a goal, but has nothing to do with the nature of the goal. Phronesis is about value judgment and is not concerned with producing things.

Another central notion of the Aristotelian philosophy is the concept of happiness or eudemonia (ευδαιμονία),[4] which, simply put, means that human beings are meant to live a virtuous and good life. It might be useful at this point to clarify the idea of the Aristotelian good life, since it is diametrically different from the modern definitions and conceptualizations of good life. The philosopher reasoned that when we say something performs well we mean it is fulfilling its purpose and the act or performance is "good." A defining feature of being human is rationality. Living in accordance with this capacity leads to a life of virtue and so a flourishing life. Therefore, a virtuous life is a good life

---

4   The correct spelling of word is eudaimonia and not eudemonia as it consists of the words "eu" (good) and "daimon" (from the ancient verb δαίω, which means I distribute luck and fate to everyone; in reality it is similar to God). In modern Greek the word deamon also has negative connotations signifying the bad demon, but we can still locate its positive roots in some words, eudaimonia being an example.

and phronesis plays an important role in our apperception of the concept of happiness (eudemonia).[5]

Modern philosophers and scholars have made a number of attempts from time to time to explain the Aristotelian phronesis. They note that the Aristotelian definition refers to a particular kind of knowledge akin to wisdom. Another part of the literature focuses on the critical and reflexive aspects of phronesis, while others argue that phronesis is about well-being, eudemonia, and moral principles. However, Aristotle's definition is not to be overridden since the philosopher was the first to introduce the term and he directs our attention to the overarching feature that the *right* individual should bring.

The philosopher pointed out that people who want to achieve wisdom need to grow properly—taking examples from the lives of others and making friends with people who are also wise—and, with wisdom, prudence, intelligence, respect, and virtuous character, they will reach the spiritual status of wisdom. Phronesis is important in a conflict situation as it allows prudent people to look beyond individual events, to think beyond common sense, and finally make decisions properly, applying wisdom for the common good.

It is true that in Aristotelian thinking, phronesis cannot be viewed separately from virtues, morality, and ethical principles, or from the collective happiness. It is important at this point to explain the link between individual and communal well-being often encountered in the ancient scripts. For the ancient Greeks, the social or political ideal was that the individual as a citizen ought to sacrifice or demote their personal happiness for the good of the communal. This ideal is based on two assumptions: 1) the impairment of the city (polis—πόλις) brings about the impairment of its citizens, and 2) personal happiness lies in the collective. Taking these assumptions a bit further, we can argue that:

- The society and the state benefit the individual, since they offer him material and spiritual goods that the individual alone cannot achieve.

- What is true for the whole is also true for the parts. A happy whole makes the people who are part of it happy. On the contrary, happy people do not always make a happy whole.

---

5   The link between virtue character and happiness has been the central preoccupation of ancient ethics and consequently the subject of much disagreement. We are not entering the philosophical debate for it extends our scope, but the reader might find it useful to refer to the hedonistic ethical theory of Epicurus and the Stoics.

- Society has a greater value than the individual. The loss of a person only temporarily affects the evolution of the society.

The issue here is not to ascertain whether the above issues are theoretically correct, but to underline the social dynamic. In our world today, how can we ensure individual and collective happiness? One way to approach this problem is by admitting (theoretically and practically) that collective happiness means happy people, not just a few happy groups, nor a practical enforcement of an ideology, a set of ideas, or a "praying" for the common good. The duty of the formal institutions is then to provide a framework within which each individual is recognized as separate from other people and feels free to express this individuality.

The Eastern Perspective

When studying the ancient scripts, it is always surprising to discover the similarities of thinking between people that lived so far away from each other and with no means of communication. The initial surprise, though, might fade away if we come to realize that all humanity shares the same concerns and that we are all driven by the same needs and desires. A bright example for exemplifying the above argument comes from the Confucian philosophy, which has had much influence on Eastern thought. The emphasis there is again on the role of moral development in determining who is fit to govern and lead society. As such, it focuses not only on adherence to rules and principles, but also the proper cultivation of moral character in all who would be fit to be governors. The two central concepts in Confucian ethics are *Jen* (pronounced "ren") and *Li*. *Jen* is considered the highest virtue and means "humanity" or "humaneness." The main characteristic of people who possess *Jen* is that they exhibit benevolence and care toward others. *Li* is the twin virtue of *Jen*, the other side of the same coin, so to speak. It is translated as propriety, benefit, order, and concrete guidance to human action. Together, these two virtues create a highly cultivated and disciplined person who behaves properly in every situation and who is motivated by deep care and empathy for people. This person is the *junzi*, or superior person. This person controls their actions, impulses, and desires in accordance with the demands of *Li* and *Jen*. As such, they exhibit a strong sense of personal power—called *te* in Confucianism— which compels people to follow their example.

This exceptional quality, combined with other knowledge and skills, makes them the ideal people to create and govern a harmonious society. For this reason, the entire corpus of Confucian teaching, texts, and traditions focused on the cultivation of moral character in people who have the intellectual capacity to learn the things necessary for government. Intellectual capacity alone for leaders and governors is not sufficient; moral character must accompany it, otherwise these governors and leaders will drive society into lawlessness and chaos.

Modern Phronesis

It has been stressed several times throughout this book that modern leaders need to act in an ambiguous environment that is constantly being changed by unpredictable external factors (such as political, economic, environmental, and technological factors), endangering the business equilibrium. It follows that leaders need to be constantly alert in the pace of modern life. Every organizational leader affects the stability of the organizational system and its symmetry depending on his/her position, experience, knowledge, behavior, and feelings. So a model modern leader would be able to identify challenges, deal with complex situations, and communicate potential problems—making them readily understood by all. They are expected to apply different practices as a solution to a problem while taking into account the needs of all those involved in the company—shareholders, managers, or employees. So that is why the ability to deal with challenges, problems, and crises is directly related to the concept of phronesis, as the latter is considered necessary when there is irreducible uncertainty and simultaneously a need for evaluation of future conditions. Phronesis then helps the leader to determine and dissect all the possibilities in order to be able to address challenges effectively. When a leader feels that they do not have control of a situation, they should consider applying different perspectives and solutions to a problem, applying wisdom and intuition to positively influence organizational members and bring them together toward a goal that will produce the desired result.

The Japanese academic Nonaka and his colleagues have been studying the subject of phronesis for some time and their studies indicate that, in the modern context, it is best defined as the experiential knowledge that enables people to make ethically sound judgments. The first application of phronesis is political; as such, phronesis is "the ability to initiate action toward the future based on universal consensus about specific goals and measures reached through the shared judgment and conviction of individuals in each concept".[6] It is similar to the Japanese concept of *toku*—a virtue that enables people to

---

6   Beiner, R. (1983). *Political Judgment*. London: Methuen & Co.

pursue the common good and moral excellence as a way of life. It is also akin to the Indian concept of *yukta*, which means "just right" or "appropriate." For instance, executives who believe that the purpose of business is to serve people and enhance society's well-being observe *yukta* and shy away from excess and greed.

The authors further argue that phronesis fits very well the demands of the modern competitive organizational environment. Without undermining the importance of profitability for a business, they specifically state that profitability should be the end result and not the primary goal. In their view, the first thing that needs to be asked is whether the organization and the leadership have a moral purpose. When interviewed for the *Harvard Business Review*, Professors Nonaka and Takeuchi used two examples from the modern business world that affirm precisely their point.[7] The first example concerns John Chambers as he was transforming Cisco from a top-down, command-and-control company to a team and collaborative one; Chambers created communities of distributed leaders, rendering Cisco the best possible model of how a large-scale company can operate. The CEO said, "We are growing ideas, but we are growing people as well. Where I might have had two potential successors, now I have 500." In a similar context, they use as a second example the best-selling car in in Mumbai, India, the Tata Nano, created by Ratan Tata (Chairman of Tata) after he visited the streets of Mumbai. Tata asked himself how he could help poor families who were exposed to the weather whilst riding their motorcycles. His solution was to produce a US$2,500 car. Thus, scholars explicitly note that today's knowledge-creating companies require a new kind of leader capable of displaying the following characteristics:

- a philosopher who grasps the essence of the problem and draws general conclusions from random observations;

- a master craftsman who understands the key issues of the moment and acts on them immediately;

- an idealist who will do what he or she believes is right or good for the company and society;

- a politician who can spur people to action;

- a novelist who uses metaphors, stories, and rhetoric;

---

7   Nonaka, I., & Takeuchi, H. (2011). The wise leader. *Harvard Business Review*, 89(5), 58–67.

- a teacher who has good values and strong principles from whom others want to learn.

Moreover, in their effort to reconstruct and modernize the concept of phronesis, the authors propose that phronesis consists of six abilities. These abilities should be considered as ideal models and not necessarily equal to each other. Instead, the authors permit a latitude and variation in their application which is basically dependent on the situation. Before moving to a brief presentation of the six abilities, it is important to note that phronesis is not a notion limited to top management. On the contrary, phronesis can be practiced by a distributed leadership, where people at various organizational levels are able to exercise it in their own situations. The abilities that constitute phronesis, according to the theoretical approach of Nonaka and Toyama, are:[8]

- The ability to judge goodness.

  At the top of the list of the phronetic components is the ability to evaluate a situation in terms of what is "good" and also apply this moral discernment based on the demands of that particular situation. As can be easily inferred, the judgment of "goodness" very much depends on individual values and, more importantly, the leader's values, given that he or she is accountable for the ethos of the organization. Consequently, a solid, philosophical foundation for their values appears to be critical, since otherwise the leader cannot be trusted to make a judgment on what is good, and a company is unable to produce value. It is important to note at this point that when the authors refer to individual values, they do not imply any pursuit of individuality. Instead, what they mean is that individual values need to be one's own and not imposed or given by anyone (individual or culture); only when the individual values are deeply rooted, believed, and tested can they help the leader to make judgments on what is commonly good in various contexts.

- The ability to share contexts with others to create *ba*.

  The authors here use the Japanese word *ba*, roughly translated as place, in an effort to depict the context in which knowledge is

---

8   Nonaka, I., & Toyama, R. (2007). Strategic management as distributed practical wisdom (phronesis). *Industrial and Corporate Change*, 16(3), 371–394.

shared, created, and implemented and every individual is accepted in respect to one's values, beliefs, and opinions. For such a context to be established, it is presupposed that leaders have developed empathetic feelings that will enable them to put themselves in the position of others (both employees and customers), which in turn will result in an increased comprehension of other's emotions and expectations. This empathetic attribute of phronesis can also cultivate imaginative capacity, in terms of quickly reading and reacting to a situation, which as everyone can imagine is of extreme importance when managing ever-changing contexts. To make their point more accessible, the authors parallel this dimension with what Souichiro Honda once said about joking: "Joking is very difficult. You have to grasp the atmosphere of the occasion and the opportunity. It exists only for that particular moment, and not anywhere else. The joke is in the timing and it doesn't work at any other moment … To joke is to understand human emotion."[9]

- The ability to grasp the essence of particular situations/things.

In this dimension of phronesis, the authors highlight the importance of being able to make sense of one's experiences, meaning that it is paramount for organizational leadership to develop the ability to grasp the essence, the true nature, and meaning of people, things, and events. The exercise of phronesis enables one to perceive beyond the ordinary to see the essence. This does not necessitate or imply any x-rays or superhuman abilities, but instead a widening in perspective. In our everyday efforts, we need to learn to make judgments and decisions taking into account both the particular and the universal, the forest and the tree simultaneously, and not being carried away from the waves of urgent or demanding problems and situations. In other words, phronetic leaders can quickly sense what lies behind the phenomena and accurately project an image of the future based on that intuition.

- The ability to reconstruct the particulars into universals and vice-versa using language/concepts/narratives.

This ability can be broken down to two components. Firstly, is the ability to conceptualize an intuitive idea, by connecting the

---

9   Honda Motor Co. Ltd. (1998). *Honda Philosophy*. Company Booklet.

"micro" concepts to a macro historical context and secondly the ability to convincingly articulate it in clear and effective language (usually in the form of vision or future scenario). As already mentioned, phronesis is more than knowing how to best behave in a particular situation. Phronesis is the ability to look at the particularities and from those generalize a universal truth that is good for the many. Hence, it requires continuous interaction between subjective insight and objective knowledge to identify the optimal way to behave.

The second component is related to how the vision will be articulated in a comprehensive, clear, and motivational manner. This component is as important as the first one, since even the most inspirational vision is unable to fulfill its potential unless it can be effectively communicated to others. In order to achieve an effective communication of the vision, the leader should possess, among other competencies, "rich imagination, especially historical imagination, and an outstanding ability to create and communicate a vision of the future that captures the imagination of others, effectively using metaphor, analogy, or simple story-telling".[10]

- The political power to realize concepts for the common good.

This ability refers to how phronetic leaders are able to create synergy inside the organization by synthesizing everyone's knowledge and efforts toward the attainment of common goals, acknowledging the different stances and conflicts of interests. This task is surely hard to accomplish but becomes easier when adopting a dialectical mentality, according to which the leader is not seeking an optimal balance between contradictions; a "both and" rather than a "either or" attitude. Thus, different or opposing opinions amalgamate to give rise to a solution that negates the dichotomy and yields knowledge. By accepting contradiction, one is able to make the decision best suited to the situation without losing sight of the goodness to be achieved.

- The ability to foster phronesis in order to build a resilient organization.

---

10 Nonaka, I., & Toyama, R. (2007). Strategic management as distributed practical wisdom (phronesis). *Industrial and Corporate Change*, 16(3), 371–394.

The last component of phronesis in the model of Nonaka and Toyama is related to the ability to promote resiliency in organizations. The issue of resilience, albeit mainly neglected in the organization behavior literature, has managed to get the attention it deserves in recent years. Adopting a cross-disciplinary approach, drawing mainly from the grounds of psychology, resilience is defined as "the developable capacity to rebound or bounce back from adversity, conflict and failure, or even positive events, progress, and increased responsibility".[11] Resilience allows not only reactive recovery but also proactive learning and growth through conquering challenges.[12]

Phronesis can function as facilitator in the process of cultivating organizational resiliency, in terms of encouraging critique and reflectiveness in organizational members. In particular, since phronesis is embedded and distributed throughout the organization, members are becoming capable of evaluating and responding flexibly and creatively to every situation, constantly keeping in mind the common good. In that way, on one hand the organization becomes more alert to upcoming threats or aversive situations and, on the other hand, more able to recover, rebound, and return to an equilibrium state since the duty of watching is not solely attributed to leadership.

However, leadership is held responsible for one task of high importance, which is setting clear examples of the phronetic way of thinking in practice. People need to learn what phronesis is through practice, accomplished in interaction. For example, Honda constantly asks its people: "What do you think?" This encourages them to think deeply about their own values in relation to the values of Honda and of society. The question also makes them think about what they want to *do* in their work at Honda in order to put their values into practice.

To summarize, for managers to be able to make the right decisions, they need to understand *why* a company exists—the *raison d'être*. Following the preceding arguments, the right judgments are guided by the individual's values and ethics. And, without a strong foundation of values, executives cannot decide what is good or bad. The cultivation of such values proves to be very important in order to develop a corporate culture and correct management in

11 Luthans, F. (2002). Positive organizational behavior: Developing and managing psychological strengths. *Academy of Management Executive*, 16, 57–72.
12 Youssef, C., & Luthans, F. (2004). Resiliency. In G. Goethals, G. Sorenson, & J. Burns (Eds), *Encyclopedia of Leadership* (pp. 1321–1325). Thousand Oaks, CA: SAGE Publications, Inc.

general, and, as we learn in early administration, their adoption is reflected in aligning business decisions to a commonly accepted purpose and creating incentives. These values are included in all of today's management manuals, but some of them may have been neglected in the recent crisis, with results that are well known to us all. The following paragraphs are dedicated to the goal of relating phronesis to other equally important concepts, namely self-awareness, authenticity, and humility, while the chapter concludes with some propositions for incorporating phronesis in today's working environment.

Phronesis as a Leadership Virtue

In ancient Greece, the ideal leader had to display phronesis (that is, good judgment about good and bad depending on the context), temperament (that is, control of desires, closely connected with the moderation and self-discipline), bravery (that is, ability to make bold but wise decisions), justice (that is, fair treatment for both supporters and opponents), and wisdom, (that is, knowledge to distinguish the facts and their cause) among others. To these skills, Chinese philosophers would add exemplary behavior, as manifested through role modeling, empathy, defined as the ability to sympathize with the feelings and needs of others, responsibility for our actions, and accountability of their impact on others.

Undoubtedly, as businesses grow big so do the problems that they face, and thus the need for phronesis becomes imperative. Also, the need arises to replace traditional leadership models, which promise a fair degree of predictability and control, with more organic and non-linear ways of thinking based on praxis. Phronesis can help managers adapt to this shift by preparing to see where things may be going next and what to do about it. In the same vein, Nonaka and Toyama[13] argue that, practitioners face a lot of problems every day and "in these situations, there is no time to do detailed analyses of the environment or resources; nor is there any guarantee that general rules that apply in the past will still apply." So, within these changing environments, we might want to start considering the potential effectiveness of leadership traits other than the traditional ones. So, for example, existential thinking and mindfulness, systems thinking or tacit knowledge might have to replace the ability to set missions or the trait of loyalty previously regarded so highly in traditional organizations.

---

13 Nonaka, I., & Toyama, R. (2007). Strategic management as distributed practical wisdom (phronesis). *Industrial and Corporate Change*, 16(3), 371–394.

To sum up, the effective functioning of an organization depends on how well the phronesis of its members is developed. The rational, ethical, and political dimensions of phronetic thinking helps leaders to form and clearly articulate overt, subjective, and intuitive ideas and also elucidate and establish the vision, the future plans, and the scope of the organization. What's more, in complex organizations, leaders need to set goals after seeking and carefully examining the incoming information. In the following chapters, we examine how three aspects viewed within the phronetic prism can help today's leaders.

Phronesis and Self-Awareness

Self-awareness has been the central theme of philosophical thinking in all ages and cultures, which means that human beings have always been characterized by the intrinsic drive to know themselves. It is defined as the capacity for introspection and the ability to recognize oneself as an individual separate from the environment and other individuals. Taking a look at the three most influential ancient civilizations, that is Indian, Greek, and Chinese, we can see that the quest for knowledge of the self was the cornerstone of their philosophies. For example, there is evidence that the people living in the area that we know now as India in 5,000 BC developed meditative techniques in order to reach the inner core of the being and get a brighter glimpse of the Self. Accordingly, in ancient Greece, Socrates expressed this idea with his well-documented "know thyself." Tu Wei-Ming, in *Confucian Thought: Selfhood As Creative Transformation*,[14] explains the moral universe of East Asia when he writes that self-knowledge "that is concerned with truly personal experience is not at all private to the individual; self-knowledge is a form of inner experience precisely because it resonates with the inner experiences of others. Accordingly, internality is not a solipsistic state but a concrete basis of communication."

This last notion is particularly important in the context of this book, since it graphically highlights that self-awareness *ends up* with the realization that human beings are interconnected and therefore we are morally obliged to consider the Other when making a decision. Without turning a blind eye to the fact that in modern populous societies, finding the balance between personal happiness and common good is often a tough job, it is imperative to keep in mind that our human essence is still the same and it will never change. As follows, the learnt apathy toward the moral scandals of modern organizations,

---

14 Weiming Tu (1985). *Confucian Thought: Selfhood as creative transformation.* New York: State University of New York Press.

the detachment from the politics, the indifference toward the poor, and so on, is actually against our nature.

However, it has been argued that, especially in relations that involve some sort of power and influence elements, the view of the self changes according to the situation, as new stimuli appear. In reality, as everything is in constant flux, it would be vain to cling to our so-thought stable personality. With each new challenge there are new elements that one learns about himself according to how the situation is dealt with. Self-concept is formed to a large extent through one's experiences and social interactions with others. When someone identifies herself and develops self-awareness in a collaborative environment, then the collective interest and vision coincides with the individual interest and vision, and thus the leader learns to act for the common good while not neglecting the personal interest. Thus, through the practice of phronesis, the leader builds self-knowledge and, given that the latter is achieved in the context of team spirit within an organizational setting, then all people involved tend to move toward a single shared goal from which all parts can benefit.

Phronesis and Humility

Humility is a virtue that one does not regularly come across, especially within a leadership context. However, in his influential book *Good to Great: Why some companies make the leap—and others don't*, Collins[15] argued that the great companies are those that have a *Level 5* leader at the helm. He reasons that the main characteristic of Level 5 leaders is that they direct their ego away from themselves to the larger goal of leading their company to greatness. These leaders are a complex, paradoxical mix of intense professional will and extreme personal humility. They produce magnificent results, but they manage to do it without gloating about anything they have accomplished, instead they are modest and always looking for better ways to do things.

Humility, in the same way as phronesis, is a meta-virtue. In essence, humility is the outcome of phronesis, as it crosses into an array of principles. For example, we can safely declare that there cannot be authenticity without humility. Indeed, leaders do not have the answers to all problems and situations and often they fail to address the right questions. Admitting this and seeking others' input requires some humility. Arrogant behaviors or "I know what to do—

---

15   Collins, J.C. (2001). *Good to Great: Why some companies make the leap—and others don't*. New York: HarperBusiness.

I did not ask your opinion" attitudes, or snobbism in lay language, may also hinder the interaction with other people; leaders should constantly keep in mind that all interactions are potential learning experiences. However, this attitude presupposes that the leader has a life stance that views all individuals as equal, not only in their natural characteristics but also in their right to fight for equality. These humble leaders will not exert superiority but will instead treat everyone with respect, regardless of the position they hold. What's more, the same respectful behavior will be manifested consistently across contexts and situations. (*The sign of the gentleman is how he treats those who can be of absolutely not use to him.*)

The good news is that humility is a virtue which can be learnt. The moment we will stop engaging in the pursuit of perfection that our competitive culture has made us think we ought to, will be the moment that we will realize that we are already perfect and that realization extends beyond our narrow self. At that time, something wonderful happens: we open up to new possibilities, as we choose open-mindedness and curiosity over protecting our point of view. We spend more time in that wonderful space of the beginner's mind, willing to learn from what others have to offer. Furthermore, the more we practice humility, the more benefits we can see. It improves relationships across all levels, it reduces anxiety, it encourages more openness and, paradoxically, it enhances one's self-confidence. It opens a window to a higher self.

In a nutshell, humble leaders are considered to be more willing to learn from their experiences and from other people and have a great desire to serve others and not just themselves. Additionally, they tend to make better decisions since they eagerly and sincerely seek advice, talk to people, work as a team—not pretending that they know everything and do not need the knowledge of others.

Phronesis and Authenticity

Organizations in today's world are faced with issues that require a new approach to the conceptualization of leadership, in terms of restoring trust, hope, optimism, and morality in the workplace. The importance for a leader to be authentic and to remain faithful to the values, emotions, beliefs, and principles cannot be overemphasized. Authentic leaders possess those cognitive and physical capabilities that enable them to know and identify the ethical values of other people, their knowledge, and their strengths.

The authentic leader is driven by a core of ethical values, formulated during childhood, which apply in the working environment. At this point the issue of what ethical values we are talking about rises. Although it has been established that the term ethical values has positive connotations (almost all of us think of ethical values in terms of good things, such as honesty, justice, and so on, at least in our own value system; even those people that are driven by rather dark motives are likely to articulate a moral code that contains words such as honesty or honor), scholars need to elaborate further as to whether the only prerequisite of an inauthentic individual is the violation of his/her integrity.

The ability to commit to moral values is directly related to practical wisdom. Those characterized as phronetic in their thinking and actions are committed to their people and cooperate with them in promoting an authentic behavior. Authentic leaders express their true self in their daily lives, without having to change, pretend, or fake, and thus live a good life surrounded by loyal people, approach eudemonia, and also exerting a positive influence on the eudemonia of their followers. In other words, authentic leaders are those who really care about others, and genuinely emphasize and manifest those sentiments at every opportunity.

Authentic leaders are likely to sacrifice their personal interests for the common good as a result of their commitment to their core values which they manifest and apply in their work. This particular type of leadership behavior establishes an ethical environment, beyond personal desires, preferences, and choices. At the same time, authentic leaders promote collective beliefs and values in the work environment that conducts and fosters team spirit and attitudes—best results and effectiveness ensue naturally. And *naturally* is the key word here; indeed, the whole process happens without coercion or fear but from an intrinsic need to serve (central concept of servant leadership).

Concluding Thoughts

A great part of the management literature has examined paradoxes in relation to organizational complexity. The theory of organizational complexity suggests that we need to conceptualize ideal leadership under a new prism. More specifically, it proposes that modern leaders need to act as a catalyst to the context and to direct learning experiences, in terms of helping organizational members to acquire *knowledge by doing*.

One may wonder how the concept of phronesis has anything to do with that. Although the general idea should be evident by now, let us just articulate some thoughts more explicitly here. Firstly, leaders or managers who want to experience a fuller, more complete and integral life might find in phronesis the meaning and the answer to existential crises that frequently emerge in the sterilized modern business environment. Secondly, the direction of leadership efforts toward the common good can make the organizational members less alienated from the end outcome (either product or service), which has been the main cause of so many psychological problems in recent times. There is an Indian proverb that says that everyone is a house with four rooms—a physical, a mental, an emotional, and a spiritual room. Most of us tend to live in one room most of the time but, unless we go into every room every day, even if only to keep it aired, we are not a complete person.

Indeed, our era is characterized by glorification and over-reliance on mental capabilities, see for example intelligence or rhetoric, while other aspects of the self are neglected to such a degree that it is obsolete or even shameful for someone to declare or cultivate spirituality. Especially in the leadership domain, no matter whether business or political, a high level of intelligence has traditionally been regarded as the number one asset for success and sustainability. But, is it really sufficient? History has provided us with far too many examples of exceptionally intelligent figures who did not use their brainpower to serve a virtuous cause but instead to initiate wars, cause genocides, polarize, and create hate. In fact, the twentieth century seems to be afflicted by inequality, poverty, and amorality, affirming Trotsky when he said that anyone desiring a quiet life has done badly to be born in that century. We argue that phronesis can be that missing piece.

Leadership cannot be cut down to a scientific process, thus degrading other aspects such as virtues, emotions, and ethics. Great thinkers whose writings have been hugely influential note that leadership skills more closely resemble artistic skills. For example, Max De Pree, in his book *Leadership is an Art*,[16] characteristically notes that "leadership is an art, something to be learned over time, not simply by reading books. Leadership is more tribal than scientific, more a weaving of relationships than an amassing of information, and in that sense, I do not know how to pin it down in every detail." In the same vein, in his essay "Political Crisis," Isaiah Berlin[17] compares good leaders to good musicians;

16 Depree, M. (2004). *Leadership is an Art*. New York: Crown Business.
17 Cherniss, J., & Hardy, H. (2013). Isaiah Berlin, in E.N. Zalta (Ed.) *The Stanford Encyclopedia of Philosophy* (Winter 2013 Edition), http://plato.stanford.edu/archives/win2013/entries/berlin/.

great leaders and artists give us perspective on our social condition (good or bad) and greater appreciation of our world, ourselves, and our choices. Moreover, the same as musicians or artists, leaders have to rely on their intuition, synthetic capacities, and sense of reality in order to create a sense of community and motivate, comfort, challenge, or excite others. In addition to the above skills, good leadership requires following proper causes and setting appropriate goals. And this is where phronesis comes in. According to Aristotle, a phronetic leader displays two characteristics; first, she or he sets virtuous goals, and, second, knows how to achieve them in fluid conditions. Phronesis and ethics are allied concepts since leaders, as agents, act, judge, interpret, and decide, drawing from their value system and sense of morality in general.

In a nutshell, phronesis should not be confused with intelligence; it is possible that an intelligent individual operates with ambitious and egoistic motives, and as such cannot be characterized as prudent. The contrary, though, is that a phronetic individual that is unintelligent is not so frequently encountered. So, phronesis, apart from its virtuous components, further assumes intellectual skills. Specifically, for phronesis to manifest, it requires cognitive and meta-cognitive skills and also the ability to think existentially.

It must have been clear thus far that those individuals who display high levels of existential thinking are considered to ponder the issues related to life, values, society, future, destiny, and so on. At the same time they are passionate and driven by their quest to pursue high goals, which will ameliorate their own and others' present situation. As such, this existential thinking is closely related to the concept of phronesis. As mentioned earlier, phronesis is the ability to see beyond the narrow reality—it cannot be separated from action and it is the key to spirituality.

Phronesis takes time to be acquired and mastered but the good news is that it can be learnt and cultivated. The ability to make a judgment on goodness depends on life experiences. The fact that work experiences and reflection upon them can be a valuable source of knowledge should not be a surprise, phronesis requires more than that to emerge. According to Aristotle, phronesis is the character embodied in a good man. To foster goodness one needs experiences as a human being in every aspect of life. Especially important are aesthetic experiences and a culture of philosophy, history, literature, and the arts, which fosters insights into historical and social situations.[18] To cultivate

---

18 MacIntyre, A. (1984). *After Virtue: A study in moral theory.* (2nd edn) Notre Dame: University of Notre Dame Press.

critical phronetic leadership, an organization must provide a mechanism for learning through high-quality experiences. And, as follows, the schools that prepare future leaders have to follow that direction. Before resistance and doubts are born to the mind of the reader, let us assure them that it can be done. Nonaka and Takeuchi, for example, launched a senior executive program in Tokyo—the whole curriculum of which consists of Aristotle, Machiavelli, Heidegger, and other classics.

Before closing this chapter, we feel that we need to articulate a question first posed by Castoriadis addressing the issue of knowledge management. The philosopher, recognizing the non-religious nature of modern societies, pondered on the need to control the dissemination of knowledge. In order to avoid any authoritative situations, he argued for the set of some principles. First and foremost, organizations and societies should not want an unlimited and imprudent expansion of production. Instead they ought to strive for a production and an economy that constitutes the *means* and not the purpose of human life. Secondly, although we aspire for the free and unconditional dissemination of knowledge, we must admit that such growth entails risks which are hard to pinpoint in advance. In order to address these risks, the Aristotelian phronesis becomes vital, for it serves to find the right answer— or about right—in situations in which a pure rational reasoning does not result or pinpoint to a single solution, but instead opens hundreds of possibilities. It becomes apparent, then, that in the current economic system, characterized by the delusion of limitless expansion, the only answer is the establishment of a process of critical reflection and open dialogue that will involve citizens in their entirety. And this, in turn, is possible only if citizens possess real knowledge and education—not just "information"—and if given real opportunities to exercise in practice their phronetic ability.

If all these seem too idealistic or too much to expect, then perhaps we need to remind ourselves of the thoughts discussed at the beginning of the chapter. Companies are assigned to create new futures if they are to survive. Analysis of raw data and deductive reasoning will not do the trick. Leaders have to employ intuitive thinking, rely on values, consider the environment (both natural and social), and then envision a new future that will take into consideration the greater good and not merely the organization's growth.

Chapter 4

Character

Introduction

If any notion is under-researched in the leadership literature, then it is definitely the issue of character. This is not the result of its insignificance but of the inherent difficulty in defining and, consequently, operationalizing it. The contemporary research studies, albeit scarce, offer useful insights into the impact of character in organizational and leadership effectiveness, but the lack of consensus on what character is seems to undermine their value. Once more, resorting to philosophy can save the day. In this chapter, we take a look at the elements that comprise character, namely values and virtues, and we bring together the attributes that define character-based leaders in an attempt to renew the interest in the issue and give it the attention it deserves within the leadership literature.

The Value of Character in Leadership

As mentioned on several occasions throughout this book, leadership literature, and consequently leadership schools and organizational systems alike, have been preoccupied with the tangible aspects of leadership, such as competencies and results—neglecting the fundamental issues that constitute leadership. However, at some point it has become evident that, despite the accumulation of many competencies and skills in leaders, leadership failures kept on happening. It was then that organizational sciences made the shift and encouraged an undertaking to investigate the inner aspects of leaders. From that endeavor, we are now able to commence an informed and constructive discussion on notions such as authenticity, phronesis, optimism, and hope as vital to a leaders' level of acceptance and followership and thereby leadership effectiveness and endurance. But, if we wanted to participate in a discussion on leaders' character, we would not have much to contribute academically. Relying on our everyday experience, we can roughly describe what character is but, more interestingly, we are capable of attributing leadership failures to its absence.

In this vein, if we were asked which is more important for leadership success—what leaders do or who they are—we would mostly likely agree on "who they are", arguing that if the character is well-established, what to do follows naturally. Character shapes how we engage the world around us, what we notice, what we reinforce, who we engage in conversation, what we value, what we choose to act on, how we decide, and how we stand as human beings and social actors in this world. And, as we shall see later on, character formulation involves values and virtues. So when character is viewed under a virtue prism, we can easily and quickly spot all those leaders who have not put any effort into building it. For example, in Greece, political leaders are undoubtedly excellent orators, prominent professionals in their field (most of them are lawyers and doctors), highly intelligent and skilled individuals, and generally display all the typical requirements for being a politician. But apparently there is something missing—the country has been so badly governed during the past decades, leading to an unprecedented debt crisis which has impacted not only its own citizens but the entire world. The Greek debt crisis has made news headlines worldwide. During the financial crisis of 2008–9, leaders from diverse sectors (business, politics, and academic) did not disclose information which could have possibly alleviated the catastrophic consequences of the financial breakdown. Instead, they remained silent and increased their bank balances at the expense of millions who were the victims of the financial crisis and subsequent recession. During that time, Goldman Sachs, for example, cashed in by betting against mortgage-backed securities. Even more disturbing than the instances themselves is the fact that almost no one was held culpable by any formal institution or political system or took the courage to take responsibility for their actions. And these behaviors and activities were, essentially, failings of character.

The Definition Problem

Just what character is has been a perennial debate in philosophy and social sciences. William James suggested that character should best be considered as those mental and moral attitudes that leave us feeling most deeply and intensely alive and vibrant.[1] It should not be surprising that achieving consensus on the definition of character is not such an easy task given that the literature review reveals overlaps with values, virtues, ethics, and personality.[2] On top of that,

---

1   James W. (1920). *The Letters of William James*, James Henry (Ed.). Boston, MA: The Atlantic Monthly Press.

2   Wright, T.A., & Goodstein, J. (2007). Character is not "dead" in management research: a review of individual character and organizational-level virtue. *Journal of Management*, 33(6), 928–958.

some definitions appear to be insufficient in describing the whole spectrum of the notion. So for example, the definition given by *Webster's Unabridged Dictionary* as "the aggregate of features and traits that form the apparent individual nature of some person or thing" ignores the fact that, historically, character had a significant social dimension. Wright and Goodstein[3] offer us a more holistic dimension when they say that "character refers to those inter-penetrable habitual qualities within individuals and applicable to organizations that constrain and lead them to desire and pursue personal and societal good." In a similar vein, Leonard saw character as "... those aspects of personality that are learned through experience, through training, or through a socialization process".[4] Sperry also offered a definition, saying that character is "that dimension of personality that describes how individuals conduct themselves in interpersonal and organizational situations and is shaped through the simultaneous development of self-identity and self-regulation".[5] Given that the literature to date has not yielded a universally agreed-on definition of character, or of character in leadership, it is logical that there is still significant work to do. In this section, we first attempt to deconstruct the elements that constitute character, namely traits, virtues, and values; we later discuss the importance of having leadership character; and we finally argue that it is time for business schools to consider the inclusion of character development courses in their curricula.

Character is ...

The current prevailing view about character is that it consists of both habitual qualities or character strengths and a second, more motivational component. Psychologists, sociologists, organizational theorists, and others who study behavior in organizations have been interested in traits, values, and virtues associated with good leadership. Virtuous leaders are influenced by their traits and values but they balance and integrate them in ways that are appropriate to the situations in which they operate. For example, while leaders may be transparent by nature, they are able to keep a confidence or secret when it is appropriate to do so. While they may be courageous, they will understand which battles to fight and which to avoid.

---

3   Ibid.
4   Leonard, H.S. (1997). The many faces of character. *Consulting Psychology Journal: Practice and Research*, 49(4), 235–245.
5   Sperry, L. (1999). The 1999 Harry Levinson Lecture: Character assessment in the executive selection process. *Consulting Psychology Journal: Practice and Research*, 57(4), 211–217.

Traits

Within psychology literature, thousands of personality traits have been identified. However, the simple juxtaposition and description of numerous personality traits did not offer any valuable insights to psychologists whereas the empirical operationalization of them was particularly complicated. Therefore, psychologists attempted to group personality traits into categories. This idea was introduced by Allport in the late twentieth century and since then has been widely adopted as evident in the numerous models proposed. In 1990, Paul Costa and Robert McCrae presented their five factor model, best known as Big 5, which has received significant support from other research and is now widely accepted among psychologists. According to the model, the five broad categories of personality traits are *conscientiousness, openness to experience, extroversion, agreeableness,* and *neuroticism.* The reason for bringing up personality traits in a discussion about character is because some traits (for example, openness to experience) reflect certain values (for example, stimulation and self-direction values) that can motivate behavioral dispositions (for example, curiosity, love of learning) that are expressions of virtues such as wisdom.[6] However, we should bear in mind that, in general, traits are not affected by situational changes, they are considered hereditary and rather fixed. But, although there is evidence (for the most part conducted in identical twins) confirming this rigid nature of personality traits, it does not account for the non-developmental and evolutionary aspect of traits. On the contrary, life experiences, counseling, and developmental exercises such as coaching, have been found to influence (positively or negatively depending on the trait targeted) the behavioral expression of specific traits. As a consequence, personality traits "lie somewhere in between habitual character strengths (or weaknesses) and motivational values in that these are not universally admired qualities, nor do they necessarily motivate the pursuit of personal or societal good, or of human flourishing."[7]

Values

Values concern what should be; they are "the normative standards by which human beings are influenced in their choice among alternative courses of action which they perceive."[8] Similarly, Kluckholm defined values as conceptions of

---

6   Crossan, M., Mazutis, D., Seijts, G., & Gandz, J. (2013). Developing leadership character in business programs. *Academy of Management Learning & Education,* 12(2), 285–305.

7   Alzola, M. (2012). The possibility of virtue. *Business Ethics Quarterly,* 22(2), 377–404.

8   Jacob, P.E., Flink, J.J., & Schuchman, H.L. (1962). Value and their function in decision. *American Behavior Scientist,* 5(9), 6–38.

what is desirable, held by either individual persons or groups, that influence courses of action and outcomes of action.[9] Rokeach further distinguished between two types of instrumental values: moral and competence—and similarly, between two types of terminal values: personal and social.[10] As a result, according to Rokeach and Beyer's widely used and commonly accepted definitions, values primarily involve an individual's opinions and beliefs about what should be or what is desirable. For our purposes here, we understand values as motivational drivers that may lead or constrain an individual to desire a particular end goal.[11] From this we can decipher that, depending on the situation, people classify their values accordingly; so, for example, conformity values such as self-discipline (for example, self-restraint and resistance to temptation) can serve as a guiding principle in one's life over stimulation (for example, excitement and novelty) values. Values are therefore the core from which we operate and hence they help cultivate particular character strengths. The behaviors associated with character strengths, in turn, forge the evolution of the values that people hold.

From the above definition, we infer that values are beliefs that people have about what is important or worthwhile to them. It is a very definitive factor that influences and guides behavior, given that people generally pursue what their values dictate. So, some of us value honesty, others creativity, others politeness, and so on. In this way, if I value harmony, I will engage in activities that promote harmony. Apparently, people do not share the same values, although culture and social environment contribute majorly in their formulation. Some people value their autonomy very highly, some value social interaction, some value the opportunity to be creative, some value work–life balance, and so on. In addition to individual differences, values usually change with life stages and according to the extent to which a particular value has already been realized. For example, in our 20s we usually value independence and non-conformity which are gradually replaced by comfort and serenity. As mentioned, social environment plays a significant role in the values that prevail in every society and community. For example, the West generally values hedonism, liberty, and well-being, while the East values order, harmony, non-violence, and equality. We could identify further levels of classification, for example, family, religion, time, and local communities, which have a strong impact on individual values.

---

9 Kluckhohn, C.K. (1951). Values and value orientations in the theory of action. In T. Parsons and E.A. Shils (Eds), *Toward a General Theory of Action*. Cambridge, MA: Harvard University Press, p. 395.

10 Rokeach, M.J. (1973). *The Nature of Human Values*. New York: Free Press.

11 Schwartz, S. (1996). Value priorities and behavior: Applying a theory of integrated value systems. In C. Seligman, J.M. Olson & M.P. Zanna (Eds), *The Ontario Symposium, vol. 8. The psychology of values* (pp. 1–24). Hillsdale, NJ: Lawrence Erlbaum.

Also applicable to our discussion on character is that people may have a set of values that are espoused but not necessarily manifest. Moreover, we frequently find ourselves in ambiguous situations where we have to act, selecting one value over another, or even worse in situations where we are forced to act in a way contradictory to our values, which usually gives rise to feelings of guilt, embarrassment, and anger. It is argued that when values are held in a strong character, the conflict does not emerge, for the individual always behaves in accordance to them.

Virtues

According to the ancient Greek philosophers, certain values and traits can be grouped under a bigger category which comprises the virtues. So, virtues are similar to values in terms of their consistency in manifestation. In the words of Aristotle, "we are what we repeatedly do. Excellence, then, is not an act, but a habit." Aristotle identified and defined 12 virtues: Courage, Temperance, Generosity, Magnificence, Magnanimity, Right ambition, Good temper, Friendliness, Truthfulness, Wit, Justice, and Practical wisdom (phronesis).

Recently, Peterson and Seligman have made an exemplary job of defining and measuring character strengths and virtues. Character strengths are the chosen or voluntary processes or mechanisms by which virtues are expressed. Drawing, on one hand, from the thousands of years of philosophical reflection and examining, on the other, the premises of psychology, theology, and sociology, the researchers argued that virtues represent abstract exemplars of good character and character strengths are the measureable group of related traits that reflect the universal virtues.[12] Their extensive literature review aimed to identify which virtues and character strengths that bring prosperity to self and society can be considered universal and constant. They ascertained 24 character strengths which can be clustered into six virtues:

1. *Wisdom*: cognitive strengths that entail the acquisition of knowledge (creativity, curiosity, judgment, love for learning, perspective).

2. *Courage*: emotional strengths that involve the exercise of will to accomplish goals in the face of opposition, external or internal (bravery, perseverance, honesty, zest).

---

12 Sosik, J.J., & Cameron, J.C. (2010). Character and authentic transformational leadership behavior: Expanding the ascetic self toward others. *Consulting Psychology Journal: Practice and Research*, 62(4), 251–269.

3.   *Humanity*: interpersonal strengths that involve tending and debriefing others (love, kindness, social intelligence).

4.   *Justice*: civic strengths that underlie healthy community life (teamwork, fairness, leadership).

5.   *Temperance*: strengths that protect against excess (forgiveness, humility, prudence, self-regulation).

6.   *Transcendence*: strengths that forge connections to the larger universe and provide meaning (appreciation of beauty and excellence, gratitude, hope, humor, spirituality).

Table 4.1   The six virtues and the vices

Virtue	Deficiency	Virtuous mean	Excess
Wisdom	Unoriginality	Creativity	Impracticality
	Closed to experience	Curiosity	Unfocused interest
	Close minded	Open mindedness	Lack of judgment
	Apathy	Love of learning	Obsessive
Courage	Cowardice	Bravery	Recklessness
	Laziness	Persistence	Zealot
	Inauthenticity	Integrity	Righteousness
Humanity	Harsh/cruel	Kindness	Obsequious
	Unfeeling	Compassion	Indulgent
	Stinginess	Generosity	Profligacy
	Socially awkward	Social intelligence	Manipulative
Justice	Treachery	Citizenship	Blind obedience
	Lack of confidence	Fairness	Undiscerning
	Unjust	Leadership	Dictatorship
Temperance	Unmerciful	Forgiveness	Pushover
	Boastfulness	Humility	Self-deprecation
	Rash	Prudence	Overly cautious
	Sloth	Self-regulation	Inflexible
Transcendence	Ungrateful	Gratitude	Suppliant behavior
	Hopeless	Hope	Foolishness
	Spiritlessness	Spirituality	Fundamentalism

Source: Adapted from Aristotle (1999) and Peterson and Seligman (2004).[13]

---

13 Peterson, C., & Seligman, M. (2004). *Character Strengths and Virtues: A handbook and classification*. Oxford: Oxford University Press; Aristotle (1999). *Nicomachean Ethics*, Book 3, Chapter 1.

According to this framework of virtues and character strengths, when a person possesses a particular virtue, we can refer to the corresponding character strengths and from there justify, on one hand, the observed behavior and, on the other, predict the future behavior.

Before moving on to provide the link with leadership, it is important to note that Aristotle could not escape from the mentality of his era concerning the golden mean and, thus, explicitly argued that virtues can become vices in their excess or deficiency. So, for example, the excessive expression of courage is recklessness while in its deficiency it is cowardice (see Table 4.1).

The Ten Virtues of a Cross-Enterprise Leader

Recently, Crossan and associates,[14] relying on the work of Peterson and Seligman, have proposed a framework for leadership character that consists of ten virtues. These are:

1.   *Judgment* allows leaders to balance and integrate these virtues in ways that serve the needs of multiple stakeholders in and outside their organizations.

2.   *Humanity* builds empathy and understanding of others.

3.   *Justice* yields decisions that are accepted as legitimate and reasonable by others.

4.   *Courage* helps leaders make difficult decisions and challenge the decisions or actions of others.

5.   *Collaboration* enables teamwork.

6.   *Accountability* ensures that leaders own and commit to the decisions they make and encourages the same in others.

7.   *Humility* is essential to learning and becoming a better leader.

---

14 Crossan, M., Gandz, J., & Seijts, G. (2012). Developing leadership character. *Ivey Business Journal*, 76(1), 3–8.

8. *Integrity* is essential to building trust and encouraging others to collaborate.

9. *Temperance* ensures that leaders take reasonable risks.

10. *Transcendence* equips the leader with a sense of optimism and purpose.

Not deviating from the Aristotelian view, the scholars provided us with detailed descriptions of what happens if the above virtues are either missed or expressed excessively. For example, collaboration in excess, ungoverned by judgment as to when it will result in benefits, leads to numerous unproductive meetings and organizational inefficiency. But without it, teamwork is difficult or impossible. Table 4.2 summarizes the outcomes of presence or absence of virtues.

Table 4.2   Good and bad outcomes of presence or absence of virtues

Virtue	Good organizational outcomes	Bad organizational outcomes
Judgment	Quality decisions, calculated risk taking, commitment, support, trust	Lack of balanced assessment of the issues leading to misinformed decisions, confusion, resistance to change
Humanity	Social responsibility, good employees relations, understanding, support	Misses critical social implications of decisions and actions, alienation of followers, lack of respect for leader
Justice	Use diversity, poor employee relations, fairness, organizational citizenship behaviors	Inequities not identified and managed thereby eroding trust, favoritism, nepotism
Courage	Decisions made under conditions of uncertainty, confidence to act, opposition to potentially bad decisions, innovation	Going along with poor decisions, satisfying rather than maximizing, moral muteness
Collaboration	Teamwork, use diversity, cross-enterprise value added, innovation, learning, affiliation, confidence	Individualism alienates potential allies, poor understanding of decisions, friction, conflict
Accountability	Ownership and commitment to decisions and their execution	Failure to deliver results and typically creates excuses for why not, shrinking of responsibility
Humility	Continuous learning, quality decisions, respect, trust	Ego-driven behavior, selective listening, difficulty admitting error or failure, arrogance, overconfidence, complacency, hubris

Table 4.2   **Good and bad outcomes of presence or absence of virtues**
continued

Virtue	Good organizational outcomes	Bad organizational outcomes
Integrity	Builds trust, reduces uncertainty, develops partnerships and alliances, promotes collaboration and cooperation	Creates mistrust, requires firm guarantees, slows down action, undermines partnerships and alliances, reduces cooperation and collaboration
Temperance	Quality decisions, reduced risk	Short-termism, inability to see the possible constraints, instant gratification
Transcendence	Focus on superordinate goals, big picture thinking, strive for excellence	Narrow aims, little inspiration, tunnel vision

Source: Crossan, Gandz, and Seijts (2012).[15]

Character Development

In this section we discuss whether courses on character building can be included in the curriculum of business programs. Alternatively, and more generally put, we are arguing whether character can be developed and taught. However, before commencing this discussion, let us clarify that our view of leadership is far away from the notions of power, fear, or obedience and irrelevant to the position of the leader. On the contrary, we view leadership as a particular type of social relationship which is characterized by a positive influence on both parties, namely the leader and the followers; the former always working toward the best self helps the latter to bring to the fore their own best self, which in turn collectively affects the organization and society. Now, although the position the leader occupies within the organization is not of the utmost importance, it goes without saying that we expect that we expect that the influence of leaders from the upper echelons will be greater.

According to ancient Greek philosophers, and especially Plato and Aristotle to whom we owe the first writings on the subject, character is not actually an area that is even closely related to education. Instead, they believed that character is no different from any other skill and as such it can be developed through habituation, that is, consistent repetition and application of the virtues comprising it over the course of one's lifetime. The more—in quantity and

---

15 Crossan, M., Gandz, J., & Seijts, G. (2012). Developing leadership character. *Ivey Business Journal*, 76(1), 3–8.

quality—virtuous acts we perform, the better and stronger the character we develop, at least according to the Greek philosophers. On top of this habituation element, Aristotle added another dimension to character development, which is social in nature. Specifically, character is formulated through interaction with others in the community context. Especially when it comes to specific virtues such as temperance, generosity, and friendliness, the individual can only develop them by frequently relating to the other members of society. Furthermore, this aforementioned social dimension has another aspect that needs to be acknowledged, which refers to observing good people doing the right thing. The argument here is that in observing others doing good we are motivated to follow their path, apparently because we also see the positive consequences of their actions.

Thus, based on all the above, arguing for character learning comes naturally. In fact, there are a number of academics from various disciplines who have proposed that "not only is character something that can be learned, but also it is the responsibility of social institutions—including educational institutions—to teach character by providing an environment that fosters virtuous behavior and where virtuous behaviors can be observed and discovered."[16] In that vein, it has been suggested that educational practices, such as role playing, collaborative learning techniques, service learning opportunities, and self-reflection exercises, which cultivate ethical culture and moral awareness, can help leaders with developing character.

How Character Develops

According to the early philosophers, character is formed through repetitive behavior and thus is more of a habit. As such, it is difficult to change—mainly because we are unaware of it—but still extremely powerful in shaping our thoughts, words, actions, and so on. The interesting thing about considering character a habit is that it has, simultaneously, a detrimental and a liberating effect. Detrimental in the sense that habits hinder the development of character and liberating in the sense that bad habits can be replaced by virtuous ones. That being said, for character to change requires an enormous effort on the part of the agent which is most of the times accompanied by a crucible event, capable of altering our mentality and replacing established values and schemata. But, effort signifies that there is room for education. For example,

---

16 Crossan, M., Mazutis, D., Seijts, G., & Gandz, J. (2013). Developing leadership character in business programs. *Academy of Management Learning & Education*, 12(2), 285–305.

when we are rewarded for a virtuous behavior, this praise will shape our character and will reinforce similar behavior. Certainly, the degree of impact of this character development process is greater when there are fewer habits, that is, in formative years, but it is not absolute, for character develops through our entire life-course. Indeed, even minor mundane incidents that can later be the subject of reflection influence character development. In this effort, we argue that formal education can play a vital and supporting role.

Both in formal business educational institutions and in everyday organizational practice, the value of character is given a secondary role compared to the importance ascribed to the development of leadership competencies and building and sustaining commitment. However, in the previous section we presented the argument that leadership character is paramount in organizational settings if the leader is to be trusted and perform effectively. Additionally, we have argued that character is not an abstract notion irrelevant to education. What follows in this section is the process, the how of character development within the business environment.

Going along with the emerging tendency of examining the organization in a more holistic and integrated way, we adopt a multi-level framework of analysis, which can make the leader acquire essential leadership qualities in three levels: self, others, and in the entire organization.[17] When it comes to the first level of analysis, leadership refers to the cultivation of positive character strengths such as humility, open-mindedness, self-awareness, and continuous learning. The interpersonal level of analysis is related to the leaders' responsibility of cultivating positive relationships with peers and followers. In the last level, the leader has to align the systems, structures, strategy, and culture to make the organization successful. Before we continue, it is important to understand that there are a number of ways that character can be developed within business educational institutions, with inclusion as a course in curriculum constituting just one way. Even simply talking about character can trigger a discussion that fosters reflection and questioning. Having clarified that, we can now turn our interest to giving some ideas on the process through which character can be developed in each of the three levels of analysis.

It is beyond doubt that the majority of business schools have given disproportional significance to cultivating leadership competencies and commitment. And although character is considered important for leadership

---

17 Crossan, M., Vera, D., & Nanjad, L. (2008). Transcendent leadership: Strategic leadership in dynamic environments. *Leadership Quarterly*, 19, 569–581.

effectiveness, we have to search quite thoroughly to locate a business program (MBA or not) that has developed a course relevant to character building. Perhaps, the reason of the paradox lies at the very nature of character, which makes it difficult to deconstruct and transfer it. Besides, character development is a life-long process, and as such does not seem to fit the fast-paced business programs, while at the same some concerns have been expressed regarding the resultant direction of teaching character. But, on the other hand, strong volition from the part of leadership (including political, educational, and organizational) combined with the technical expertise of modern instructional designers can give rise to programs that would provide leaders with the means to become better, character-wise. Warren Bennis addressed the role of individual responsibility in becoming a better leader when he said: "The leader never lies to himself, especially about himself, knows his flaws as well as his assets, and deals with them directly. You are your own raw material. When you know what you consist of and what you want to make of it, then you can invent yourself."[18]

In this regard, character can be developed in two ways; either explicitly through designated courses or implicitly by infusing character development in all courses. So, for example, character can be the subject of dedicated courses that emphasize its significance in leadership and its development. Specifically, it has been found that courses that put the emphasis on the processes of self-awareness and reflection, apart from making the future leaders thoughtful and mindful, have an overall impact in organizational effectiveness. Indeed, cultivating self-awareness makes the leader alert and prepared to continuously doubt the habitual behaviors and question the established ways of achieving things, trying to find better solutions. In their exemplary paper, Crossan and associates argued that there are at least four types of formal educational techniques that can be employed for teaching character in business schools, namely increased training in ethical decision-making, experiential methods that challenge implicit cognitive biases, reflection exercises designed to surface dissonance between the type of person one is and the type of person one might wish to become, and mentoring.[19] The first technique uses as a means the case study methodology; by working on case studies, leaders encounter real case scenarios and put themselves in the position of the decision-maker. With the appropriate guidance, leaders increase their levels of awareness which in turn impacts the ability to recognize the morality and feasibility of the alternatives. However, this ensuing increased

---

18 Bennis, W. (1989). *On Becoming a Leader*. New York: Random House Business Books.
19 Crossan, M., Mazutis, D., Seijts, G., & Gandz, J. (2013). Developing leadership character in business programs. *Academy of Management Learning & Education*, 12(2), 285–305.

awareness of the different ethical frameworks does not guarantee the leader will eventually choose to act in a virtuous manner when in a real situation.

To deal with this, educational systems are responsible for providing the necessary link with experience. This can be accomplished by transforming the current educational paradigms from mainly didactic to more experiential. Experiential learning is a process of making meaning and learning from direct experience and through reflection on doing. Although primarily a theory of learning relevant to schools, experiential learning in business has become very important. It is considered among the most powerful teaching and learning tools available. The most cited model is the one proposed by Kolb according to which learning is happening by following four steps that do not end up linearly but instead form a loop (see Figure 4.1).[20]

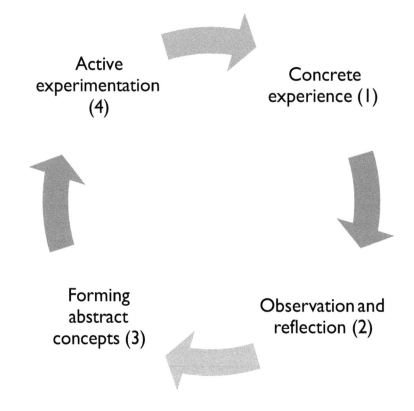

Figure 4.1   **Kolb's experiential learning cycle**

---

20   Kolb, D.A. (1984). *Experiential Learning: Experience as the source of learning and development.* Englewood Cliffs, NJ: Prentice-Hall, Inc.

Kolb's four-stage learning cycle shows how experience is translated through reflection into concepts, which in turn are used as guides for active experimentation and the choice of new experiences. The first stage, *concrete experience* (CE), is where the learner actively experiences an activity such as a lab session or field work. The second stage, *reflective observation* (RO), is when the learner consciously reflects back on that experience. The third stage, *abstract conceptualization* (AC), is where the learner attempts to conceptualize a theory or model of what is observed. The fourth stage, *active experimentation* (AE), is where the learner is trying to plan how to test a model or theory or plan for a forthcoming experience.

In recent years, educational experts have developed a series of techniques that facilitate experiential learning. Relevant to management education are role-playing, the use of simulations, and on the job training. Most importantly though, and in line with the premises of experiential learning, character can be developed through fostering reflective activities. So, through writing a journal, reflecting on activities and actions, and discussing with peers, students engage in a form of inductive reasoning where abstract concepts are connected to real-life examples.[21] Moreover, business schools can plant the seeds for appreciating the value of reading literature in enhancing reflection on ethical situations.[22] These techniques allow one to move from the question, "What is the right course of action in this situation?" to a more character-based framing, such as, "What kind of person do I want to be?"[23]

As already mentioned, character can be implicitly cultivated, but this implies an even more radical transformation of educational systems than merely adding a course on character development. Indeed, it requires the employment of staff that genuinely believes, embraces, and actively supports the pedagogical role of professors. This further means that they understand their responsibility to contribute to the development of character which at the same time implies a degree of culpability when character fails. Granted not all faculty members are aware, willing, or confident in extending beyond the limits of transferring knowledge but perhaps that could be another sign that educational systems are calling for a change; educators should also be selected on the basis of character given that schools are vital contributors of the moral degree of society.

---

21 Hill, A., & Stewart, I. 1999. Character education in business schools: Pedagogical strategies. *Teaching Business Ethics*, 3(2), 179–193.
22 von Weltzien Hoivik, H. (2009). Developing students' competence for ethical reflection while attending business school. *Journal of Business Ethics*, 88(1), 5–9.
23 Audi, R. (2012). Virtue ethics as a resource in business. *Business Ethics Quarterly*, 22(2), 273–291.

Now, turning our attention to the remaining two levels of analysis, we argue that there is much that business leaders can do in order to develop leadership character in others. In particular, leaders are responsible for creating meaningful and honest relationships with peers and followers within every level of organizational context (that is, within departments, between departments and organization as a whole). Accepting their role as models of behavior, they should expect that what they do, value, appreciate, ignore, and notice has a significant effect on the other organizational members. So, drawing from the Aristotelian view that good character is developed by observing good people doing the right thing, it becomes evident that what we do defines who we are. At the organizational level, we cultivate character by creating an environment that fosters virtuous behavior. Again, learning is accomplished by doing; if leaders want an ethical workforce, then values need to be addressed daily and explicitly within the organization. Setting an ethical code of conduct is not the most appropriate method to get there; instead, character should permeate the organization's structures, strategies, rules, and procedures (that is, recruitment, selection, training, organizational design, culture shaping, and so on).

Concluding Thoughts

"When it comes to leadership, competencies determine what a person can do. Commitment determines what they want to do, and character determines what they will do."[24] Taking this thought further, what we will do is very much dependent on who we are. And that is why leadership character has been rediscovered and reappreciated in our days. Modern business environments require leadership at all organizational levels, rendering those with leadership character responsible for creating positive relationships, achieving results and long-lasting success. Recognizing the importance of leadership character, it is quite surprising that it has not been given the appropriate attention, either in organizational settings or in research efforts. Moreover, character development was until recently a terra incognita in business schools, an argument that stands on its own regarding the respect it was given. To be fair, though, there is a renewed interest in the significance of values—personal and organizational—in leadership development, but until they become an integral and inseparable part of a general character-based leadership, the approach is bound to fail.

---

24 Crossan, M., Gandz, J., & Seijts, G. (January/February 2012). Developing Leadership Character. *Leadership*. Retrieved 20 December 2013 from http://iveybusinessjournal.com/topics/leadership/developing-leadership-character#.Ut0PZ7STuNI.

Thus, appreciating character within the leadership field, people are able to lead in a more holistic way as they learn to develop the parts that constitute it. It is important to note once more that character is not an either–or construct (someone has it or not) and surely not an end state. Life gives countless opportunities for deepening and strengthening our character, especially crises. But, if leaders are given the provisions, then the number of failures might decline.

To sum up, in addition to competencies and commitment, there is an element, rather neglected so far, that is paramount for leaders' success and organizational sustainability—leaders' character. When the individual is motivated and reinforced to work on his/her character, there are effects which extend beyond the narrow boundaries of the self. In fact, in this journey of becoming a better person, the leader entices other people into developing their own character. As a result of this, organizations and societies perform at the highest level.

Chapter 5
Integrity

Introduction

Earlier in the book we mentioned that business studies have recently experienced a conceptual shift from a utilitarian (cost–benefit) or Kantian (rule-based) theoretical approach aimed at answering the question, "What is the right thing to do?" to a more virtual-based approach seeking to answer the question, "What kind of person ought we to be?" Current paradigms are moving away from searching for the optimal decision for a particular situation, focusing instead on dispositions that constitute good character and looking for positive patterns of behavior that can be sustained across time and situations.[1] Following this line of thinking, in this chapter we discuss the virtue of integrity, in terms of its meaning, value, and usefulness in organizational settings.

In Search of a Definition

It is true to such a degree that it is almost axiomatic that if people have integrity, we can usually trust them. So, if we design organizations with integrity, it is reasonable to expect that people would trust them too. Integrity is a quality that we seek and appreciate in all personal relationships and social interactions, but its value is magnified even more in leadership exchanges. A great number of organizational theorists and practitioners acknowledging the importance of integrity in leadership note that any lack or compromise of integrity endangers the survival and future of the organizations. And since survival depends very much on the development and establishment of trust, reciprocal respect, and commitment in all possible combinations (for example, organization–customers, leaders–followers, followers–leaders, and so on), integrity is considered the notion that generates those, among many other, positive organizational effects.

---

1 Chun, R. (2005). Ethical character and virtue of organizations: An empirical assessment and strategic implications. *Journal of Business Ethics*, 57(3), 269–284.

But what is the real meaning of integrity? We all talk about integrity but we do not seem to agree on what it is. According to the CEO of General Electric, Jack Welch:

> *Integrity is something of a fuzzy word. People with integrity tell the truth, and they keep their word. They take responsibility for past actions, admit mistakes and fix them. They know the laws of their country, industry and company—both in letter and spirit—and abide by them. They play to win the right way, by the rules.*[2]

In a similar vein, integrity has been described as the direct reverse or opposite of hypocrisy in that it considers internal consistency as a virtue, and suggests that parties holding apparently conflicting values should account for the discrepancy or alter their beliefs. Dr Kenneth Bra states, "It's self-evident that a hypocrite is unqualified to guide others toward attaining higher character. No one respects a person who talks a good game but fails to play by the rules. What a leader does will have a greater impact on those he or she wishes to lead than what a leader says. A person may forget 90 percent of what a leader says but he or she will never forget how the leader lives."[3] Although in the same general direction, the two aforementioned quotes take a different standpoint on integrity; the first focuses on honesty and responsibility while the second puts the emphasis on the consistency between words and actions. And, this is only the preview of the confusion that surrounds integrity. It appears that scholars, although agreeing on the positive effects of integrity, do not share the same ideas about its components or even the nature of the concept (that is, is it a personality trait, or a virtue, is it different from character, or is it just a behavioral manifestation of honesty?). As follows, the literature on integrity is at the very least varied.

It should not come as a surprise, then, that this variety in the definitions of integrity has resulted in an analogous confusion within leadership domain. And although the outcomes of integrity are again recognizable (for example, it is found to be a prerequisite for trust development and followership), we have not established undisputable correlations or determined the degree of impact or even begun to understand the process through which followers attribute integrity to their leaders. Specifically, integrity has been associated with values, virtues, and character, while at the same time has been given a

---

2   Welch, J. (2005). *Winning.* New York: Harper Collins.
3   Boa, K. (2010, April 5). The process of integration [Blog Post]. Retrieved 15 April 2013 from http://www.kenboa.org/blog/2010/04/05/the-process-of-integration/.

few classifications, such as emotional or behavioral integrity. Moreover, when scholars discuss integrity, they also refer to ethics, morality, honesty, probity, authenticity, and fairness; despite the conceptual proximity between the notions, in order to clear up this confusion surrounding integrity, we need to address it as a separate concept detached from other closely related ideas.

In response to this relative lack of explanations, it has been proposed that an excellent way to approach integrity is by considering it as a virtue which, as noted earlier, can be considered as the main component of good character.[4] Adopting this stance about integrity, we further agree with the idea that integrity is best considered as a super-virtue, or meta-virtue, implying a synthesis of many other virtues. Such an approach results in two types of advantages; first, the relationship with other virtuous moral constructs makes more sense and, secondly, it enables us to draw upon thousands of years of philosophical reflection given that integrity has been traditionally viewed as a virtue.

To summarize, the notion of integrity suffers a great deal, mainly due to definition problems which consequently lead to confusion in empirical studies. Now, trying to correlate an ill-defined concept with no established measurement instrument with the already perplexing and vast leadership literature is a task bound to be unfulfilling and inconclusive. As a result, research on leadership/ followership and integrity is ambiguous and quite puzzling, not providing any explicit correlations with other constructs, such as honesty, contentiousness, fairness, or trustworthiness. So, before we begin a discussion on leadership integrity, it is imperative to illuminate the different theoretical approaches and philosophical directions that characterize integrity and agree to a definition that we believe best grasps its essence. In this endeavor, we employ the framework of Palanski and Yammarino[5] who, reviewing the relative literature, came up with five aspects of integrity: wholeness, consistency of words and actions, consistency in adversity, being true to oneself, and integrity as a moral/ ethical behavior.

1.   Integrity as wholeness.
      The word integrity is derived from the Latin *integer* which means wholeness or completeness. Based on this literal meaning of integrity, a great part of theorists understands integrity as wholeness, completeness, or undividedness. In turn, wholeness refers to an

4   Palanski, M.E., & Yammarino, F.J. (2007). Integrity and leadership: Clearing the conceptual confusion. *European Management Journal, 25*(3), 171–184.
5   Ibid.

inclusive coherence of various parts and of the relationship dynamics between those parts. Needless to say, these parts may not always be constant and hence the relationship between them is called dynamic. Thus, when we are talking about integrity from this wholeness sense, we suggest integration of parts into a whole. When used in this sense, integrity is becoming synonymous with character.

This unifying process results in an integrated self with balanced connections between the different parts.[6] However, achieving this equilibrium is an unending task and far from being straightforward or smooth. The process implies an individual who, with awareness, willingness, and control, deals with multiple values in "a sort of multivalency, resulting in integration of the self and its environment—including its organizations and society as a whole."[7] It is important to underline that, apart from working toward a coherent self, integrity as wholeness involves a social dimension, in terms of social roles and interactions with other people and institutions. This social dimension of integrity renders the achievement of equilibrium (or wholeness) even more difficult as the probabilities for the individual to encounter situations or people that will test his/her integrity are high. But, when the institution, the role, or social environment is compatible with one's own values and virtues, the likelihood of slips lowers. This last sentence, though, triggers the beginning of a long discussion regarding whether integrity can be attributed in non-conflict conditions.

2.   Integrity as consistency of words and actions.
      This aspect of integrity, also known as behavioral integrity (BI), is the most frequently encountered in leadership literature and is defined as consistency between what one does and what one says. In the words of Charles Watson:

      There is wholeness in what a person with integrity says and does. There is consistency between his actions and what he purports to honor. He pursues his aims along the high road and is uninterrupted and undiminished by temptations for quick and easy personal gain.[8]

---

6   Wolfe, D.M. (1988). Is there integrity in the bottom line. In Suresh Srivastva (Ed.), *Executive Integrity: The Search for High Human Values in Organizational Life* (pp. 140–171). San Francisco, CA: Jossey-Bass.
7   Wolfe (1988), p. 166.
8   Watson, C.E. (1991). *Managing with Integrity: Insights from America's CEOs*. New York: Praeger, p. 171.

It is important to note that behavioral integrity should not be equated with simple promise-keeping; it is far more subtle as it extends to include consistency between espoused values and actual displayed values.

3. Integrity as being true to oneself.
    This type of integrity is closely related to the notions of self-awareness or authenticity. When integrity is employed in such a manner, it means that someone is acting, behaving, and communicating in accordance with one's own conscience. For example, an individual with integrity, under this spectrum, would be someone who selects a workplace compatible with his values, against any external pressures (that is, financial considerations or family pressures). Accordingly, individuals who readily resign from an environment the moment a value discrepancy takes place or comes to their attention, can be considered as integral.

4. Integrity as consistency in adversity.
    This aspect of integrity is not conceptually far away from the one previously mentioned, but it inserts an important variable in the equation, which is the presence of a situation of adversity or temptation. In fact, many theorists argue that, for integrity to manifest, there has to be a condition where consistency between words and actions is not granted or at the very least easily attained. The central idea here is that we cannot make any judgments on others' integrity unless we see how they will behave in the face of adversity, temptation, or challenge. The rationale behind this aspect is that perceptions of integrity are necessarily accompanied by a choice between two (or more) courses of action. Following, if there is not choice, then there can be no integrity attributions. So, integrity is indicated under conditions of adversity or temptation possibly resulting in great cost to oneself. Consequently, if the agent chooses personal pleasure or immediate gratification instead of sticking with principles, integrity cannot be their attributable characteristic. Carter aptly notes that "we admire those who stand up for their beliefs when they have something to lose."[9]

    On other occasions, integrity has been understood as resisting temptation, but this definition of integrity is rather passive and negative. In reality, integrity is and should be associated more with

---

9   Carter, S.L. (1996). *Integrity*. New York: Harper Collins, p. 23.

proactive behavior and action. To put it more simply, someone who does not act or is simply not doing wrong is not necessarily a person with high integrity. On the contrary, someone who errs may have much more integrity than someone who is just holding back. Imagine, for example, a situation where a leader of a manufacturing company finds out that its suppliers are employing under-aged children; if the leader has been positioned against child labor and campaigns for childhood respect, even if the violation is not happening within his/her organization, by not breaching the collaboration deal (if not going public), she or he cannot be considered as having integrity.

5.   Integrity as moral or ethical behavior.
       Integrity is largely associated with the issue of morality or ethics. In fact, both in everyday interactions and in scholarly literature, when we characterize a person of high integrity, we usually mean that she or he is a highly ethical or moral individual. And, given the inherent social nature of both ethics and morality, a great number of researchers imply a normative dimension of integrity. Without doubting that there is not, we must acknowledge that integrity cannot be equated with the simple absence of unethical or immoral behavior or with just following socially acceptable norms. Instead, integrity is more associated with better-than-expected ethical or moral behavior.[10] But, as usually is the case, when we add the issues of morality and ethics into any discussion, things are bound to get complicated. Indeed, we cannot ignore the relativism that accompanies them. As a result, integrity is not an indisputable or objective characteristic but may vary across cultures and situations. However, this view, if taken further, may imply that the attribution of integrity lies solely in the perception of others, which might mean that a person can be seen as having integrity by a number of people but not by others. In an attempt to reconcile this view, it has been proposed that integrity should be based on an objective, morally justifiable set of values.[11] But again, history has shown that any attempt to comprise an exhaustive and generally accepted list can be problematic.

---

10 Palanski, M.E., & Yammarino, F.J. (2007). Integrity and leadership: Clearing the confusion. *European Management Journal*, 25(3), 171–184.
11 Parry, K.W., and Proctor-Thomson, S.B. (2002). Perceived integrity of transformational leaders in organisational settings. *Journal of Business Ethics*, 35(2), 75–96.

Integrity as a Virtue

As discussed above, considering integrity as a virtue may help us clear up the fuzz. In the previous chapter we directed our attention toward the issue of character defined as a set of dispositions that make us behave in a systematic manner; we also mentioned that what distinguishes good from bad character is that the "good character" is constituted by virtues. And, virtues are "those dispositions which not only sustain practices and enable us to achieve the goods internal to the practices, but will also sustain us in the relevant kind of quest for the good, by enabling us to overcome the harms, dangers, temptations, and distractions which we encounter, and which will furnish us with increasing self-knowledge and knowledge of the good."[12]

However, integrity has a much broader sense compared to other virtues such as courage, reverence, or humility, the meaning of which is somehow narrower. Under integrity are grouped a number of other qualities of character, such as honesty or authenticity; the role of integrity is to bring those qualities into a unity, so that there is no inconsistency between them and the character of the person is unaffected by any turbulences. Moreover, considering integrity as a virtue saves us from the danger of misconceiving a bad character as integral. Indeed, the inherent morality that is attached to virtues leaves no room for an individual to be considered as having integrity even if there is no instance of inconsistency between what she or he says and does.

Integrity in Leadership

Hardly anyone would doubt that when we characterize a leader as having integrity, we mean it as a compliment; we attribute positive characteristics such as honesty, transparency, and determination and we imagine that these leaders would generally do good for the organization, in terms of treating their employees fairly, non-discriminatorily and honestly, not stealing from the organizational resources, revealing the true financial data to the shareholders, and standing behind the quality of the products or services, just to give a few examples. Apparently, such a leader is expected to function with integrity across different situations and to all people. And, although we are not in a position to know exactly the time and process through which followers form impressions on leaders' integrity, we can be fairly sure that integrity in

---

12 MacIntyre, A. (1984). *After Virtue*. (2nd edn). Notre Dame, IN: University of Notre Dame Press, p. 219.

organizational settings has a number of positive effects, among which the most discussed are followers' satisfaction and trust, and perceptions of increased leadership effectiveness.

The theoretical analysis of the preceded sections can help us disentangle integrity from a leadership perspective. So, within the leadership domain, integrity has been defined as "commitment in action to a morally justifiable set of principles and values."[13] Within this definition an objective perspective of integrity is assumed in which moral justification is based on a universal truth or reality rather than a merely agreed-upon set of morals and values by an individual or a group. However, although many organizations and leaders are aware of, and officially convey, the importance of integrity in their formal communications (for example, mission statements), their cultures and individual leaders may not reflect this awareness.

Moreover, based on the feature of inclusion mentioned earlier, an important note needs to be made about integrity and leadership in that the former does not simply mean avoidance of doing the wrong thing, but also doing the right thing. Most of the times, non-action is perceived as a way of acting or as a conscious stance. In that vein, when leaders are perceived as having low integrity, it is either because they succumbed to an unethical or immoral behavior or the followers perceived an inconsistency between the espoused values and actions or words of their leader. To make our point more articulate, in Greece, the members of the parliament are given the constitutional right to vote for, against, or present (neutral) in any bill or legislation. So, if a political leader decides to go for neutral on a budget bill that reduces money for education, this may still give the impression of low integrity to the citizens that voted for him after he committed to schools' funding during the electoral campaign.

However, we do not insinuate that leading with integrity is easy. It could not be, for leadership itself is not easy. It is more of a complex relationship than a singular concept and, apart from power, vision, or motivation, it definitely involves emotions such as fear, love, pride, and resentment. Taking this stance, several authors, recognizing the role of emotions in leadership and accepting that integrity as a holistic phenomenon cannot exclude emotions, have suggested that emotional integrity may be a more appropriate notion in order to fully grasp the leadership phenomenon. Suffice to say, any crack in this

---

13 Becker, T. (1998) Integrity in organizations: Beyond honesty and conscientiousness. *Academy of Management Review*, 23, 154–161, 157–158.

emotional relationship is perceived as betrayal, an admittedly strong emotion that seems to go to the very core of our being and is hard to recover from.

Robert C. Solomon, in accordance with that line of thinking, suggests that emotional integrity is a kind of super-virtue, in terms of a synthesis of emotions that are in harmony.[14] Harmony is not a term lightly chosen by the author; borrowing from music, harmony is a state that signifies the combination of contrasted elements: a higher and a lower note. It is not the mere accumulation of pleasant elements, but the finding of the right balance between the counterpoints.[15] But, it is crucial to understand that this balance is not a compromise between personal and behavioral aspects of the self, which implies a dichotomy between the inner and outer self. In fact, Solomon, renouncing Cartesian dualism and mirroring Wittgenstein, claims that integrity is "a public phenomenon, even when it is private."[16] In line with the group of psychologists who do not distinguish "inner" emotional states from their "behavioral" expression, the author attaches importance to the social dimension of integrity. Again, the emotional integrity of a leader is manifest in complex and difficult-to-handle situations which are bound to generate mixed feelings. And since a leader typically experiences equivocal emotions and decisions, emotional integrity includes the notion of self-mastery, which contains the awareness of emotions and the cultivation of the *right* ones, which bring us back to the issue of harmony.

Moreover, accepting that integrity is a concept that signifies the whole and, secondly, that it is best considered as a virtue, the author further argues that integrity implies a reciprocal relationship with something larger than the person—the society, the community, the humanity, the cosmos. Besides, virtue is socially valued, bound to culture, politics, and institutions. The ancient Greeks used to say that "To lead a good life and to be a good person, one must live in a great city." Accordingly, from the other part of the globe,

---

14 Solomon, R.C. (2005). Emotional leadership, emotional integrity. In J.B. Ciulla, T.L. Price, & S.E. Murphy. *The Quest for Moral Leaders. Essays on leadership ethics* (pp. 28–44). Cheltenham, UK: Edward Elgar.

15 In music, counterpoint is the relationship between voices that are harmonically interdependent (polyphony), but independent in rhythm and contour. It has been most commonly identified in classical music, developing strongly during the Renaissance and in much of the common practice period, especially in Baroque music. The term originates from the Latin *punctus contra punctum* meaning "point against point." In its most general aspect, counterpoint involves the writing of musical lines that sound very different and move independently from each other but sound harmonious when played simultaneously). Retrieved 1 May 2014 from https://www.princeton.edu/~achaney/tmve/wiki100k/docs/Counterpoint.html.

16 Solomon, R.C. (2005). Emotional leadership, emotional integrity. In J.B. Ciulla, T.L. Price, & S.E. Murphy. *The Quest for Moral Leaders. Essays on leadership ethics* (pp. 28–44). Cheltenham, UK: Edward Elgar.

Confucius used to say that prosperity lies in virtue, integrity, and a real sense of community. From that, we can decipher that a leader with integrity, in the same way as a phronetic leader, pursues something larger than ephemeral pleasures or personal ambitions; instead, they direct their efforts into formulating a worthwhile purpose which through fostering a sense of partnership is shared among all organizational members.

Organizational Outcomes

Integrity is a notion highly valued and desirable in business settings. Numerous scholars call for business to elevate leaders who are "authentic, people of the highest integrity, committed to building enduring organizations… We need leaders who have a deep sense of purpose and are true to their core values."[17] But why is integrity important for leadership? In this section we will present the results of selected studies that explore the effect of leaders with high levels of integrity to various aspects of organizational reality.

A number of studies have documented the positive impact on subordinates' workplace attitudes as an effect of perceptions of high integrity of their leader. Before we move on, it is useful to clarify that most studies employ as the main operational variable the perceived behavioral integrity (PBI) of the leader, a concept that can be distinct from the actual measure of leader integrity. So, Simons[18] defines PBI as the "perceived pattern of alignment between an actor's words and deeds. It entails both the perceived fit between espoused and enacted values, and perceived promise-keeping." Behavioral integrity is viewed as a trait ascribed to the target in the present, drawn on an evaluation of past words and deeds, describing a pattern of alignment between another's espoused and enacted values, but without taking into account the morality of the espoused values and principles (for example, we are not thinking that a leader has integrity even when they keep their promise that over time will not be kept). Trust, in contrast, looks forward to future decisions, with behavioral integrity being a key antecedent.[19]

In this regard, research has exhibited particular interest as can be manifest in the number of recent studies that attempt to provide a link between behavioral

---

17 George, W. (2003). *Authentic Leadership: Rediscovering the secrets to creating lasting value.* San Francisco, CA: Jossey Bass, p. 5.

18 Simons, T. (2002). Behavioral integrity: The perceived alignment between managers' words and deeds as a research focus. *Organization Science,* 13(1), 18–35.

19 Ibid.

integrity and trust, but admittedly our knowledge is far from complete. Although the tendency of all research findings is toward a positive correlation between the two constructs, the diversity of definitions about trust (they have focused on intent, on risk and vulnerability, on ethical justifiability, and/or on value congruence) make the deductions difficult. In general, though, it appears that high levels of leader behavioral integrity directly impact followers' sense of certainty that the leader will act as promised.[20] Similarly, leader integrity has been associated with follower commitment under the similar justification that the leader deserves this kind of attachment.

Another widely cited organizational outcome of leaders' integrity is related to follower satisfaction with the leader and satisfaction in the job. Specifically, research findings seem to be homogenous when they suggest that leader integrity has positive effects on follower job satisfaction levels in terms of creating an ethical and fair working environment.[21] More specifically, an ethical culture has been found to contribute positively to the level of employees' loyalty toward the organization, which further means that they unleash their productive and creative potential within the working environment and boost performance.[22] Moreover, presuming that creativity is not merely dependent on individual traits, but is also facilitated by the social and cultural context, Palanski and Vogelgesang argue that leaders' integrity seems to positively affect followers' creative thinking by fostering a sense of psychological safety among subordinates which in turn encourages risk taking.[23] This argument is further supported by studies that look at the issue from the reversed side; for example, workers are less satisfied with workplaces characterized by injustice, less productive in such settings, and more likely to leave them.

In addition, there have been a number of studies that indicate that leader integrity influences the levels of follower integrity. Looking at the main premises of charismatic, transformational, ethical, or authentic leadership, this happens because leaders function as role models to their followers by setting a personal example;

---

20 Simons, T.L., & McLean-Parks, J. (2000). The sequential impact of behavior integrity on trust, commitment, discretionary service behavior, customer satisfaction, and profitability. Paper presented at the Annual Academy of Management Conference, Toronto, ON.

21 For example, Innocenti, L., Peluso, A., & Pilati, M. (2012). The interplay between hr practices and perceived behavioural integrity in determining positive employee outcomes. *Journal of Change Management*, 12(4), 399–415; Prottas, D.J. (2013). Relationships among employee perception of their manager's behavioral integrity, moral distress, and employee attitudes and well-being. *Journal of Business Ethics*, 113(1), 51–60.

22 Rossouw, G.J. (1997). Business ethics in South Africa. *Journal of Business Ethics*, 16(14), 1539–1547.

23 Palanski, M.E., & Vogelgesang, G.R. (2011). Virtuous creativity: the effects of leader behavioral integrity on follower creative thinking and risk taking. *Canadian Journal of Administrative Sciences*, 28(3), 259–269.

so, if leaders have integrity, then according to research findings, subordinates tend to follow their example and work toward achieving a better moral self. In addition, there is some evidence that the integrity of the leader has an impact on hiring and firing processes, meaning that, on one hand, a leader with high integrity tends to attract people with a similar integral tendency and, on the other hand, tends to repel those who do not share that tendency.[24]

Furthermore, motivational theories can also be summoned to provide another angle of explanation concerning the relationship between leaders' perceived integrity and increased levels of followers' performance. So, for example, we can draw the instrumentality factor of the Vroom's expectancy theory, according to which individual effort is dependent on the individual's belief that will receive a reward if the performance expectation is met.[25] As such, if the employee views the leadership as untrustworthy or unethical, it is highly probable that he or she will exert less effort as a result of the disbelief that the management will follow through with the promised rewards.

Although all research findings indicate that leader integrity is positively associated with increased organizational performance, we should not forget that leader integrity is not a necessary condition for success. On the contrary, if the work gets done, integrity, albeit desirable, is not always granted. Moreover, given that the leader performs multiple leadership roles and engages in a wide repertoire of behaviors (that is, behavioral complexity),[26] the risk of being seen as spineless[27] is quite big. Moreover, scholars and practitioners must be very cautious and learn to cultivate the ability to utilize those definitions of integrity that do not leave issues open to misinterpretation; for example, we would not say that a leader has integrity if what she or he claims lacks moral base even if there isn't any observed inconsistency between words and deeds.

Concluding Thoughts

Integrity is part of one's character, comprised of a number of discrete virtues, such as behavioral consistency between words and actions, espoused values

---

24 Schneider, B., Goldstein, H.W., & Smith, D.B. (1995). The ASA framework: An update. *Personnel Psychology*, 48(4), 747–773.

25 Vroom, V.H. (1964). *Work and Motivation*. New York: Wiley.

26 Hooijberg, R., & Quinn, R.E. (1992). Behavioral complexity and the development of effective managers. In R.L. Phillips & J.G. Hunt (Eds), *Strategic Management: A multi-organizational-level perspective* (pp. 161–176). New York: Quorum,

27 Weick, K. (1978). Spines of leaders. In M.W. McCall & M.M. Lombard (Eds), *Leadership: Where else can we go?* (pp. 37–61). Durham, NC: Duke University Press.

and enacted values, stability over time and across situations, avoidance of hidden agendas, and acting morally, transparently, and sincerely driven by internal values. As already mentioned, there is a growing interest within leadership scholarship in leaders' integrity; the catalyst for this research focus seems to be precipitated on one hand by the increasing instances of misconduct, scandals, corruption and, on the other, by the positive outcomes, in terms of job satisfaction, trust building, and efficiency, linked with organizations led by integral individuals. As has eloquently been noted, integrity is "a relational unity that makes a differentiated constellation of parts held together as one."[28] It is foundational to any viable organization because by definition organization is differentiation integrated[29] (ibid.). Indeed, one may generalize to say that integrity is the viable "holding together" of any system.

If we wanted to keep a few things in mind from the above analysis, the first important point is that integrity is a virtue naturally uncompromising and thus rarely—if ever, to be honest—restored. Without implying that the other virtues can be easier in their reset, it seems that the nature of integrity leaves little space for forgiving. Indeed, whereas a single action may undermine the sense of integrity, there is no single action (or, indeed, any number of actions) that will definitively re-establish a person's integrity. This stands as a very good explanation for those individuals who exceed in defending their—oftentimes— apparent and undeniable misdeeds and corruption; they know (or sense) that even a single slip can utterly destroy a lifetime of good deeds and even raise serious doubts about the purity of past intentions, behaviors, and actions. This becomes apparent when we think of integrity as the fragmentation of the self, that is that break in wholeness explained before, that is required by saying one thing and doing another. Therefore, lack of integrity is not simply a breach between action and language, but an enormously complex form of self-deception for integrity is not something a person "has" or "does" (or does not do). It is a way of being.

However, one can object by arguing that no individual and what's more no leader, especially in the corporate level where power and fame can be distracting, is perfect. In fact, we encounter integrity violations in sectors that are permeated by a strong ethical and moral code, and where forgiveness is in their "mission statement," such as religious organizations, but still, those leaders were not given a second chance. Take, for example, John Friend,

---

28 Srivastva, S., & Barrett, F.J. (1989). Foundations for executive integrity: dialogue, diversity, development. In Srivastva, S., et al. *Executive Integrity: The search for high human values in organizational life* (p. 5). San Francisco, CA: Jossey-Bass.
29 Ibid, p. 291.

an admittedly charismatic leader who thought of a patent yoga system which became something like an empire. The system he developed was intelligent and it helped—physically, emotionally, and mentally—millions of people all over the world. He advocated ethics as the core of his system and said repeatedly that he wanted to have an ethics evaluation. But when an ethics committee was established, he refused to go through it. He was accused of sexual relations with his students when he advised for moderation and frozen pension contributions when he urged for transparency and not to steal. He impacted thousands of lives negatively. His mistakes and resulting implosion of the system caused loss of income and reputation for those who depended on him, believed in and supported him for nearly two decades.

The above example illustrates the point that we think is endemic to leadership. Given that leaders exist beyond corporate organizations and scientific efforts are directed toward generalized conclusions, followers' expectations about leaders' efficiency are below their expectations about their wholeness; wholeness as a person, wholeness in the sense of being an integral part of something larger than the person—the community, the corporation, society, humanity, the cosmos. But, let's make it clear that integrity has nothing to do with perfection nor can be considered as an exceptional virtue. But, it is essential to a decent life and what endures through change and trauma. Especially in the business context, where the conditions are complex and the interests conflicting, integral leaders are expected to function as the glue between the opposing parts. And though integrity does not guarantee success, there can be no success without it. On top of that, there is sufficient research evidence to argue that integrity is one of the determinate factors for organizational prosperity and a climate of trust. It has also been found that the perceived integrity of US presidents is positively correlated with their approval ratings.[30] Moreover, ethical leadership renders integrity an explicit part of the leadership agenda through communication, role modeling, and rewards and sanctions[31] (Brown & Trevino, 2006).

To summarize, the majority of, if not all, charismatic and transformational theories argue that leaders act as role models for the organization. That literally means that organizational members observe and are influenced by the values and behaviors of leaders. Adding that leaders are responsible for the kind of culture that will prevail within the organization, we can safely assume that

---

30 Newman, B. (2003). Integrity and presidential approval, 1980–2000. *Public Opinion Quartery*, 67(fall), 335–367.

31 Brown, M.E., & Trevino, L.K. (2006). Ethical leadership: A review and future directions. *Leadership Quarterly*, 17(6), 595–616.

leaders who display high levels of integrity are more likely to attract and develop followers who also display high integrity. Finally, we have argued that integrity is best seen as a virtue, and as such its effect in the organization is amplifying. In other words, it seems logical to purport that the positive effects of leadership will be amplified when the leader has high integrity.[32]

32 Palanski, M.E. (2007). Integrity and leadership: A multi-level conceptual model and partial test. PhD Dissertation, Graduate School of Binghamton University, State University of New York.

Chapter 6

Solitude as a Leadership Meta-Competence

Introduction

Undoubtedly, leadership behavior and effectiveness is strongly related to leaders' traits and the dynamic process of their psychological functioning. As Warren Bennis said:[1]

> *Leaders are made, not born and made more by themselves than by any external means ... No leader set out to be a leader for you but rather to express him/herself freely and fully ... Becoming a leader is synonymous with becoming yourself ... The leader's work is inner work.*

Manz, by developing the concepts of self-leadership and inner leadership describes some quite important dimensions of the leader's inner work.[2] Kets de Vries and Shekshnia[3] suggest that each leader adopts a particular leadership style and develops certain competencies (but not others) because of his or her inner theater. In spite of the significant progress that has been made in leadership theory, Pratch and Levinson[4] are right in arguing that research, by neglecting important issues concerning the personality, fails to address the relationship between overt, easily observed traits, behaviors, and decision styles of executives and their inner worlds. In practice, Kets de Vries maintains that "many executives don't pay much attention to their inner world." So if we want to go deeper into our understanding of the leadership phenomenon, we have to investigate and invent new unexplored paths. For example, trait

1   Bennis, W. (1989). *On Becoming a leader*. New York: Random House Business Books.
2   Manz, C.C. (1986). Self-leadership: Toward an expanded theory of self-influence processes in organizations. *Academy of Management Review*, 11(3), 585–600.
3   Kets de Vries, M.F.R., & Shekshnia, S. (1998). Vladimir Putin, CEO of Russia Inc. The legacy and the future. *Organizational Dynamics*, Special Issue on Russian Leadership, 37(3), 236–253.
4   Pratch, L., & Levinson, H. (2002). Understanding the personality of the executive. In R. Silzer (Ed), *The 21st – Century Executive* (pp. 49–73). San Francisco, CA: Jossey-Bass.

theories have to examine the psychological functioning as a dynamic process in order to provide insights into the integrity of personality and the cohesion of an individual's value system. We have to explore more the soul, heart, mind, and the unconscious and irrational behaviors of the leaders. We have to answer why some people are disposed toward specific competencies as, for example, passion, edge, energy, focus, vision, integrity, courage, values, ideas, self-awareness, or emotional intelligence, and why others are not. Which process of the "inner theater" and which "inner disciplines" lead to the development of these competencies?

In this chapter, we will try to contribute to the understanding of the inner world of the leader by using the concept of solitude which up to now has been neglected by the leadership research and literature. Solitude is a vital social phenomenon, a familiar positive experience for anyone, and a popular concept in poetry, music, and literature. Before we continue, it is essential to differentiate the concept of solitude from loneliness. Solitude is considered a positive experience as opposed to the negative experience of loneliness, with its painful nature and its contribution to psychological disorders such as schizophrenia and depression.[5] As Paul Tillich aptly writes: "English language has wisely sensed the two sides of being alone. It has created the world 'loneliness' to express the pain of being alone and it has created the world 'solitude' to express the glory of being alone."[6] The French writer Collette wrote: "There are days when solitude is heavy wine that intoxicates you, others when it is a bitter tonic and still others when it is a poison that makes you beat your head against the wall."[7]

Historically, solitude has been associated with beneficial outcomes. Religious leaders, such as Moses, Buddha, and Jesus, famous writers, such as Thoreau and Kafka, and also scientists have resorted and appreciated solitude when in a creative phase.[8] For example, Pablo Picasso said that "without great solitude no serious work is possible," while Thomas Edison affirmed that "the best thinking has been done in solitude."[9] Similarly, Goethe acknowledged that "one can be instructed in society but can only be inspired in solitude."[10]

5   Burke, P.J. (1991). Identity processes and social stress. *American Sociological Review*, 56(6), 836–849.

6   Tillich, P. (1963). *The Eternal Now*. New York: Charles Scribner's Sons.

7   Phelps, R. (1966). *Colette: Earthly paradise, An autobiography*. New York: Farrar, Straus, and Giroux, p. 139

8   Storr, A. (1988). *Solitude. A return to the self*. New York: Free Press.

9   Zubko, A. (2003). *Treasury of Spiritual Wisdom (A collection of 10,000 powerful quotations for transforming your life)*. New Delhi, India: Motilal Banarsidass Publishers Pvt. Ltd., p. 441.

10   Goethe, J.W. (2011). *Maxims and Reflections*. CreateSpace Independent Publishing Platform.

Recently, in the literature of psychology, some authors have empirically supported the positive effect of solitude, particularly to engage in self-selected activities free of social circumstances and expectations. According to Cynthia Crossen of *The Wall Street Journal*,[11] 31 percent of US residents wanted more time to be alone, whereas only 6 percent wanted less. Additionally, the Wilderness Act of 1964 (USA public law 85-577) recognized the importance of solitude as a soul phenomenon.

References to solitude exist among organizational leaders. C. Handy sustains that "a leader must have the capacity of being alone, because he has to be out front. Few will thank the leader when things go right, but many will blame the leader if things go wrong. Great leaders have to walk alone from time to time."[12] Collins Powel said:

> *Harry Truman was right. Whether you are a CEO or the temporary head of a project team, the buck stops here. You can encourage participative management and bottom-up employee involvement, but ultimately the essence of leadership is the willingness to make tough unambiguous choices that will have an impact on the fate of the organizations. Even as you create an informal, open, collaborative culture, prepare to be lonely.*[13]

In this chapter, we introduce the concept of solitude and analyze it in respect to leadership relationship. In spite of its importance, solitude has not been given the attention it deserves in leadership literature, thus creating a gap we aspire to bridge. As follows, firstly we start by defining solitude as a voluntarily activate mental and psychological state and as a positive and constructive experience for the leader. Secondly, drawing mainly from the disciplines of psychology and philosophy, we discuss some of the positive effects of solitude, such as self-reflection, self-awareness, self-leadership, decision making, creativity, and moral thinking, on leader's competencies. Finally, we will present the empirical aspect of solitude as manifest in a qualitative and quantitative study employing middle and upper-level managers.

---

11 Crossen, C. (1996). *Solitude is in short supply*. Retrieved 12 January 2010 from http://www.southcoasttoday.com/apps/pbcs.dll/article?AID=/19960312/LIFE/303129955.

12 Handy, C. (1996). The new language of organizing and its implications for leaders. In F. Hesselbein, M. Goldsmith, & R. Bechard (Eds), *The Leader of the Future: New visions, strategies and practices for the next era* (pp. 3–11). San Francisco, CA: Jossey Bass.

13 Smeby, J.L. Jr (2005). *Fire and Emergency Services Administration: Management and leadership practices*. Ontario, Canada: Jones and Bartlett Learning, p. 23.

The Concept of Solitude

When examining the relevant literature there seems to be a consensus about what solitude is. The scholars usually define it as a state into which the individual enters consciously and intentionally in order to improve and embellish the quality of their thinking and also engage in reflection on experiences and actions. It is important to emphasize that solitude refers to a condition that has not been socially imposed or enforced but instead is the result of voluntarily activation. When that activation will take place rests upon the discretion of the agent, and it usually takes the form of temporary withdrawal from social action, often facilitated by conditions of increased anonymity, and/or limited demands for social interaction. As follows, the individual does not resort to solitude as a result of their inability or unwillingness to cope with the everyday pressures and demands but instead because they value and recognize its positive impact on inner and outer directed action. Furthermore, a great many of the existing definitions agree that in the state of solitude the individual chooses to step away from any form of social interaction in order to create the space for mental stimulation and centering.

If we turn our attention to the philosophical definitions of solitude, we notice that they integrate three components, namely physical isolation, social disengagement, and reflection. In the words of Philip Koch, "solitude is, most ultimately, simply an experiential world in which other people are absent. Other people may be physically present, provided that our minds are disengaged from them; and the full range of disengaged activities, from reflective withdrawal to complete immersion in the tumbling rush of sensations, find their places along the spectrum of solitudes."[14]

In line with these definitions, we do not regard aloneness as a prerequisite for solitude. On the contrary, solitude can be experienced even in situations that do not exclude the presence of others, as long as demands for interaction are not pressing and there is room for anonymity (see, for example, retreats or taking group meditation classes). In fact, so far the empirical evidence on managerial reflection corroborates the aforementioned argument, meaning that the context in which solitude takes places functions as the mental space for reflection upon critical aspects of their role.

As already mentioned, solitude is a positive and constructive experience, diametrically distinct from the notion of loneliness. The difference lies in

---

14   Koch P. (1994). *Solitude. A philosophical encounter.* La Salle, IL: Open Court, p. 15.

the fact that the individual seeks solitude purposefully for reflection whilst the connotations of loneliness are rather negative. Specifically, loneliness mainly denotes an individual with personal or social deficiencies. It further characterizes a condition of emotional distress that arises when the person experiences or perceives alienation, rejection, disaffection, indifference, and separation from other social partners.[15] Koch provides an insightful comment when he classifies loneliness as an intrinsically painful emotion whereas solitude is better regarded as an open state. A last note that needs to be made before we delve into the analysis of the concept concerns the directionality of solitude. Solitude is not guided exclusively by inner directionality, but by the integration between inner and outer directionality, the use of reflection for inner self-regulation for regulation of subsequent action.

The Generic Benefits of Solitude

As noted, although research on solitude is limited, there are studies that have searched its effects on the soul, heart, and mind of the individual (see Table 6.1). From the naturalistic perspective, solitude has been viewed as a state of contemplative reflection and is related to mental and emotional health. Hammit suggested that wilderness privacy, which is a state of solitude, has a number of positive effects that include cognitive freedom, self-evaluation, personal autonomy, self-identity, emotional release, and reflective thoughts.[16] Hollenhorest and Jones have argued that solitude brought on by psychological detachment from society serves two primary functions: 1) affirmation of individual will and self-determination; and 2) cultivation of the inner world of the self, hence contributing to the search of meaning, happiness, self-awareness, and emotional maturity.[17] And advocating the benefits of solitude, the authors, who lent themselves to the humanistic approach, suggested that solitude should not be seen as a state reserved only for mentally or otherwise privileged individuals, but rather a state that every individual who seeks to realize one's own potential has the right to experience. They believed that solitude is related to the inner world of self-reliance and ingenuity.

---

15 Barbour, J.D. (2004). *The Value of Solitude. The ethics and spirituality of aloneness in autobiography.* Charlottesville, VA: University of Virginia Press.

16 Hammit, W.E. (1982). Cognitive dimensions of wilderness solitude. *Environment and Behavior,* 14(4), 478–493.

17 Hollenhorst, S., & Jones, C. (2001). Wilderness solitude: Beyond the social–spatial perspective, USPA, *Forest Service Proceedings,* RMRS-P-20, 56–61.

Table 6.1   Generic benefits of solitude

- Cognitive freedom
- Inner peace and security
- Emotional release
- Self-determination
- Cultivation of inner world—introspection
- Reflection
- Creative thinking—imagination
- Spirituality
- Intimacy

From an existentialist point of view, solitude represents the experience of discovery of one's personal truth and reason for being. Kierkegaard[18] observes that there are three dimensions in each human being, namely the aesthetic, ethical, and religious dimension. In line with the movement he represents, Kierkegaard considers this aspect of existence as a form of solitude, which is an inevitable condition (treaty) of life and is tightly connected with the experiences and the questions that we pose regarding to life and death. Solitude constitutes a state in which by searching for the "truth" of our existence we discover our own selves. The philosopher develops the idea that people's lives are authentic and integrated only when they make their choices and act by having conscience of their freedom, responsibility, and "solitude." On the contrary, according to Heidegger,[19] when the individual allows in others to determine the values and limits in which they will act, then the meaning and the authenticity are being lost in their lives. Therefore, for Heidegger, solitude constitutes an existential (ontological) necessity.

Solitude is seen as a necessary state by Moustakas as well, who adopts a phenomenological perspective and suggests that solitude constitutes the ideological "shelter" within which the individual executes the process of recognition and acceptance of his or her existence, discriminating from the others in order to live authentically and to be effective in his or her relations with the others.[20] The individual "enters" into a situation of solitude when he feels the need to make the right choices or to review somebody from the sectors of his life. According to this point of view, solitude constitutes a necessity for the achievement of a person's authenticity of communication as well as well as

18 Kierkagaard, S. (2005). *Fear and Trembling.* London, UK: Penguin Books Ltd.
19 Heidegger, M. (2001). *The Fundamental Concepts of Metaphysics: World, finitude, solitude.* Bloomington, IN: Indiana University Press.
20 Moustakas, C. (1961). *Loneliness.* Englewood Cliffs, NJ: Prentice Hall Inc.

for more general growth as a human being (existence). Through solitude people achieve integration and ego deepening, by discovering and determining the values and the meaning of their existence in regard to the other. It is important to note that Moustakas assumes that "aloneness" is a dimension of solitude, the experience of which he sees as a "peaceful" inner process that provides an opportunity for the individual to wonder about harmony in life, about the relations with the other, and to contemplate answers to questions that concern the human existence.

Other authors have also similar orientations. Merton stresses the importance of solitary life, along with the necessity for quiet reflection in an age when so little is private.[21] Storr also notes that the experience of having others around us may be over-valued in contemporary society.[22] He points at the over-estimation of the importance of social relationships as sources of happiness in modern society, and notes the under-estimation of the significance of the "inner mind" separated from the influence of external attachments. Storr believes that the capacity to be alone is one aspect of an inner and solitude provides a means of becoming aware of one's deepest needs, feelings, and impulses—a road toward self-realization. For this reason he suggests that the capacity to be alone should be seen as having equal importance to the capacity of the individual to be involved in social relationships. In support of Storr's point, psychological scientists have come to conclude that solitude provides an opportunity to engage in self-selected activities relatively free of social encumbrance and expectations (Burger, Larson).[23] They argue that we need time alone as a relief from social pressures that will allow personal, spiritual, mental health self-restoration, personal growth, and creative development. Similarly, Koch identifies the following benefits of solitude: 1) freedom from social norms and other constraints that control interpersonal life; 2) attachment of self; 3) attunement of nature; 4) reflection including introspection, recollection, and contemplative analysis; and 5) creativity.

Long and Averil summarize the benefits of solitude in four areas.[24] The first area is related to freedom of choice with respect to actions and thoughts.

21 Merton, T. (1968). *Thoughts in Solitude*. New York, Doubleday.
22 Storr, A. (1988). *Solitude. A return to the self*. New York: Free Press.
23 Burger, J.M. (1995). Individual differences in preferences for solitude. *Journal of Research in Personality*, 29(1), 85–108; Larson, R.W. (1990). The solitary of life: An examination of the time people spend alone from childhood to old age. *Developmental Review*, 10(2), 155–183.
24 Long, C., & Averill, J. (2003). Solitude: an exploration of benefits of being alone. *Journal of the Theory of Social Behavior*, 33(1), 21–44.

They distinguish between "negative" and "positive" freedom. Negative freedom pertains to freedom from constraints, while positive pertains to the ability to engage in desired activities. The second area concerns the issue of creativity. They support that solitude facilitates the imaginative involvement in multiple realities, enables self-transformation by self-examination and creative re-conceptualization of self, and leads to the reconstitution of cognitive structures by the emergence of new conceptual associations and combinations. Thirdly, the authors argue that, in spite of the apparent paradox, solitude implies intimacy by involving feelings of connection with the other people. Lastly, solitude enhances spirituality, defined as the ability to contemplate one's place in the universe and one's thoughts or desires. Spirituality is also closely related to a feeling of intimacy or connectedness to others and to the world. Long and Averil provided some empirical evidence for the above suggestions. In an empirical study they found solitude to be related to important cognitive and emotional outcomes such as problem solving, inner peace, self-discovery, creativity, intimacy, and spirituality.[25]

Considering the above-reviewed literature, the following conclusions can be drawn regarding the positive effects of solitude: At the level of mental and psychological well-being, solitude can contribute toward inner peace, inner security, intimacy, and spirituality. However there is a second, more subtle, level in which solitude functions; it prompts self-discovery, self-evaluation, self-determination, reflection, imagination, creative thinking, decision making, learning, and connecting with others. In general, therefore, the limited extant literature from the fields of naturalistic studies, philosophy, and psychology, as well-known facts from the lives of influential individuals in human history, suggest that solitude is a state that can substantially contribute to the cultivation of many of the intelligences described by Gardner, and especially the logical–mathematical, the intra-personal, the interpersonal, and the existential.[26]

Solitude as an Enabler of Effective Leadership

According to Value-Based Leadership Theory, which integrates the prominent theories of leadership (transformational, charismatic, visionary, authentic, ethical and path–goal theories), leaders infuse collectives, organizations, and work with ideological values by articulating an ideological vision, a vision of a better future, to which followers are claimed to have moral right.

---

25 Ibid.
26 Gardner, H. (1993). *Multiple Intelligences: The theory in practice.* New York: Basic Books.

Table 6.2   The positive effects of solitude experience on leadership

- Enhance leaders' self-awareness and self-leadership
- Facilitates leaders' envisioning
- Enhance leaders' learning an self-development
- Facilitates creative and right thinking, decision making and problem solving
- Develops leaders' authenticity
- Enables leaders' morality
- Reflection, imagination, creative and right thinking

They are characterized by a passionate commitment to their vision and values, self-confidence, strong conviction in the moral correctness of their beliefs, a sense of responsibility disposition, integrity, a concern for others and for consequences of their own actions, and critical self-judgment. In addition, and as enablers of the above, appear to be leadership traits or competencies such as self-awareness, self-regulation, emotional stability and maturity, and emotional and social intelligence. Lately, special emphasis has been given to a leader's ability to execute and achieve results, which requires willpower, energy, focus, persistence, courage, and strength (see Table 6.2). All these competencies are linked directly or indirectly to the "self-leadership" processes, including the learning process. It is true that "he that would govern others first should be master of himself."[27] Also it is true that a "leader's work is inner work," a work that the leader does within him or herself by the dynamics of cognitive processes.[28] As already mentioned, each leader adopts a particular style and develops certain competencies because of his or her inner theater. If we wish to analyze solitude as a leadership meta-competence we have to identify its positives effects at least on some of all these cognitive processes.

Solitude Enhances Self-Awareness

The widely cited notion of authentic leadership begins with knowing yourself deeply ("know yourself," Greek Ancient Quote). Leaders must struggle with their identities: what type of leader am I, what do I want my legacy to be, what values do I want to ensure or embody in my business? Kets de Vries suggests that healthy people have the capacity for self-observation and self-analysis

---

27 Philip Massinger (1583–1640), British dramatist. repr. in (1976) *The Plays and Poems of Philip Massinger*, in P. Edwards and C. Gibson, Timoleon, in *The Bondman*, act 1, sc. 3 (1624).
28 Mackoff, B., & Wenet, G. (2000). *The Inner Work of Leaders: Leadership as a habit of mind*. New York: AMACOM.

and they are highly motivated to spend time on self-reflection. Self-awareness, as a deep understanding of one's emotions, strengths, weakness, limitations, and one's values and motives is considered as a fundamental dimension of emotional intelligence. Solitude, by creating the states of dissociation, freedom, inner peace, inner security, and spirituality facilitates the process of introspection, of search, and of understanding of the deeper genuine self. In solitude, the leader can listen to his inner voice, to connect with himself at a deeper level, to find his own heart, to understand his soul, his deepest or hidden desires, emotions, feelings, and impulses. It is easier for him to search for the meaning of life, his place in the universe, and the legacy he wishes to live behind. Goleman and his associates maintain that "perhaps the most strong (though least visible) sign of self-awareness is a propensity for self-reflection and thoughtfulness. Self-aware people typically find time to reflect quietly often by themselves. Many outstanding leaders in fact bring to their work life the thoughtful mode of self-reflection that they cultivate in their spiritual life. For some this means prayer or meditation for others it's a more philosophical quest for self-understanding."[29] Storr suggested, that by extracting us from our customary social and physical contexts or at least altering our experience of them, solitude can remove those people and objects that define and confirm our identities and facilitate self-examination, re-conceptualization of the self, and coming to terms with change. Through this quest and self-discovery, the leader defines and realizes his own identity, acquires a sense of his destiny, a sense of purpose and meaning that he wants most to pursue in and through his life. Thus, he understands and keeps alive the answers to fundamental questions such as, Who am I? Where do I come from? Where do I want to go? Through this introspection, self-analysis, and self-reflection the leader creates the necessary background to make fundamental choices and commitments concerning his values, vision, and goals which form a source of will power, the force behind energy and focus. William George, former chairman and CEO of Medtronic, supports this argumentation:

> *Self-awareness and other emotional intelligence skills come natural to some less so to others—but these skills can be learned. One of the techniques I found most useful in gaining deeper self-awareness is meditation ... I have meditated 20 minutes, twice a day ever since. Meditation makes me calmer, more focused and better able to discern what's really important. Leaders by the very nature of their positions are*

---

29 Goleman, D., Boyatzis, R.E., & McKee, A. (2002). *Primal Leadership: Realizing the power of emotional intelligence*. Boston, MA: Harvard Business School Press.

under extreme pressure to keep up with the many voices clamoring for their attention. Indeed many leaders lose their way. It is only through a deep self-awareness that you can find your inner voice and listen to it.[30]

Solitude facilitates a leader to "find his voice," which is absolutely critical to becoming an authentic leader. The leader, in solitude, by listening to his inner voice, establishes or revitalizes his values, something that Tichy considers to be one of the most crucial and toughest jobs of the leader.[31] Establishing values is not a matter of instant discovery and process. It needs a continuous reflection and interpretation of the leader's external and internal world. The leader often has to confront dilemmas, doubts, conflicts, and competing values and goals. According to cognitive dissonance theory, individuals experience anxiety-inducing cognitive dissonance when their self-evaluative cognitions and behavior are in conflict with each other. Leaders must go through an act of inner consensus building in which they resolve their own conflicts. Bruch and Ghoshal state that many managers report a disconnection between their feelings and their rationally developed goals.[32] In this case, strong psychological conflicts and a sense of discomfort result, blocking purposeful action. Therefore leaders have to align their emotions and thoughts about their values and goals. The authors suggested specific strategies for this alignment which require an "inner work" of the leader which is facilitated during a state of solitude. Specifically they suggest: freeing yourself of external expectations—such as taking some time off work to think and reflect, which can help you pinpoint your hidden emotions and honestly answer for yourself what course you wish to take.

Solitude Facilitates the Leader's Envisioning

Secondly, the leader, based on the above in a state of solitude, finds it easier to conceive and formulate vision for a better future which will express his aspirations, his hopes and his dreams, and will incorporate his values. More precisely, solitude is necessary for the process of visualization through which the leader could simplify his vision into a vivid mental picture. This process of mental imaging is very useful, if not necessary, because the clearer and more vivid his picture, the stronger his passion and personal commitment (attachment) to his vision. Besides that, the leader needs a vivid mental

---

30 George, W. (2004). Find your voice. *Harvard Business Review*, 82(1), 35.
31 Tichy, N. (1997). *The Leadership Engine*. New York: Harper Business.
32 Bruch, H., & Ghoshal, S. (2004). *A Bias for Action*. Boston, MA: Harvard Business School Press.

picture since this facilitates communication, understanding, and acceptance of his vision by his followers. Experienced top athletes consider that mental imagery contributes enormously to their success and so they practice it often. Koestenbaum maintains that visioning means to be at home within the infinity of inner space and time.[33] Solitude may help to achieve access to and control over inner space and time. "Visioning is the ability to shift from the natural to the reflective attitude from being who you are to reflecting who you are, from acting out who you are to observing and evaluating who you are, from seeing the world from within your subjective ego to seeing yourself objectively within the world, from acting to examine your action." ... "Visioning is enhanced by an attitude of non-attachment, of being detached from emotional identification with the issues at hand. Non-attachment is a fundamental skill required for the creation of visionary leadership intelligence."[34]

Solitude Helps the Leader's Focus and Commitments

Solitude reinforces a leader's focus and commitment to goals and long-term objectives by simplifying them into a vivid mental picture and by intentionally channeling all activities toward achieving the desired goal. Bruch and Ghosal suggest that focus requires "time to reflect regularly on your own behavior and being willing and able to choose what you do and not do each day."[35] Apart from that, solitude helps leaders manage their painful emotions and inner tensions which may decrease their energy, their focus, and commitment to vision and goals. Heifetz and Linsky suggest that the leader has the need of a sanctuary, a place of reflection and renewal, where he can listen to himself and reaffirm his deeper sense of self and purpose:

> In turbulent seas of a change initiative, you need to find ways to be steady and stabilize yourself. First, you must establish a safe harbor where each day you can reflect on the previous day's journey, repair the psychological damage you have suffered, renew your stores of emotional resources and re-orientate your moral compass. Harbor might be a physical place, such as the kitchen table of a house, or a regular routine such a daily walk through the neighborhood.[36]

---

33 Koestenbaum, P. (2002). *Leadership: The inner side of greatness*. San Francisco, CA: Jossey-Bass.
34 Ibid.
35 Bruch, H., & Ghoshal, S. (2004). *A Bias for Action*. San Francisco, CA: Harvard Business School Press, p. 23.
36 Heifetz, R., & Linsky, M. (2002). A survival guide for leaders. *Harvard Business Review*, June, 65–67.

Bruch and Ghosal found that effective leaders know exactly how to process their painful emotions and inner tensions:

> *Most of them could name certain activities that help them cope with their strong emotions. One manager told us about his garden which had a strong stabilizing effect on him. During difficult periods, he spent long hours there, often talking to himself, about what bothered him. He knew that gardening would restore his inner balance so that could plan his next steps.*[37]

The same authors stress that a leader, by reflecting and visualizing his former success and the ways in which he overcame certain obstacles, can reinforce his self-confidence, his sense of competence, and strengthen his courage.[38] Storr states that the capacity to be alone is one aspect of an inner security.[39] Koestenbaum states that to be courageous is to be prepared for the isolation of leadership."[40] Courage requires inner security. "You must have power that comes from being comfortable with isolation so that you will be centered enough to wait patiently for results."[41]

Solitude Enhances a Leader's Learning

By facilitating reflection as a conscious act, solitude can contribute to the learning process and to a leader's self-development. Initially, through a self-awareness process and the formation of the "ideal self," a leader can realize the gap which, according to Senge, is a source of creative tension for personal development.[42] Also, solitude facilitates the cognitive processes which are created by consciously thinking about his experiences and rolling them over in his mind in order to draw lessons from them. Storr[43] feels that "thinking is predominantly a solitary activity although others may be present when an individual is concentrating upon his thoughts." Besides that, solitude contributes to the articulation of a leader's stories through which he better understands himself, he learns and he teaches his followers.

---

37 Bruch, H., & Ghoshal, S. (2004). *A Bias for Action.* San Francisco, CA: Harvard Business School Press, p. 36.
38 Ibid.
39 Storr, A. (1988). *Solitude. A return to the self.* New York: Free Press.
40 Koestenbaum, P. (2002). *Leadership: The inner side of greatness.* San Francisco, CA: Jossey-Bass, p. 150
41 Ibid.
42 Senge, P. (1990). *The Fifth Discipline.* New York: Doubleday/Currency.
43 Storr, A. (1988). *Solitude. A return to the self.* New York: Free Press.

In accordance with the abovementioned ideas, solitude contributes positively to the cognitive processes through which the leader acquires his self-identity, self-awareness, and forms his values, his vision, and his priorities. We can then assume, indirectly—that is, through these processes, that observed leader's traits—such as willpower, passion, self-confidence, strong conviction in his beliefs, courage, persistency, determination, focus, consistency, integrity, emotional stability, and emotional intelligence—are influenced.

Solitude as an Enabler of the Right Thinking

In order to manage the contradictions, paradoxes, and ambivalences required to shape the future of the organization, and to realize that vision and achieve outstanding performance, leaders have to think big, think the right questions, and think ahead. They must do this by constantly seeking and evaluating new information and knowledge and by searching for insights, not only about the micro and macro issues of markets, technologies, and people, but about the wider world around them. Leaders have to generate ideas, to make choices and decisions in order to realize vision and achieve outstanding results. Challenging of the status quo, change, innovation, and entrepreneurship require creativity, thinking the unthinkable, intuition, systems thinking, analysis, synthesis, inductive and deductive reasoning, judgment, cognitive complexity, independent thinking, and tough decisions. These cognitive functions require contemplative reflection, concentration of the thought, attention, seriousness, inner peace, inner security, tranquility, and time. Usually, these are not understood within the pressing "work environment." Many managers are distracted by the thousand tasks that they juggle each day. According to Bruch and Ghoshal, 40 percent of managers are characterized by business and non-action.[44] Besides the organizational and social context, in combination with the established schemata, scripts, mindsets, and knowledge structures favor "in the box thinking" and stereotyped ready solutions. On the contrary, solitude could care and contribute positively to the crucial cognitive functions of the leader. Through solitude leaders unleash their cognitive resources from the distractions by the myriad tasks that they have to cope with every day. Daft and Lengel argue that:

> Becoming mindful means eliminating noisy mind chatter and fragmentation so that you can hear your subtle inner voice. The daily practice of contemplation or meditation may help unlock your subtle

---

44 Bruch, H., & Ghoshal, S. (2004). *A Bias for Action*. San Francisco, CA: Harvard Business School Press.

> *forces of creativity and independent thinking, generate assumptions,*
> *challenging questions and connect you with fresh insights and deeper*
> *truths ... Leader mindfulness means being willing to stand apart*
> *... to determine your course by your inner rudder rather than by an*
> *external radar.*[45]

In the same spirit, Bruch and Ghoshal[46] support that it is imperative for a leader to take his or her time to step back and reflect.

If we look for more specific positive contributions of solitude in the cognitive functions of a leader we could, on the basis of the existing bibliography, sustain the following. First of all, the state of freedom that a leader experiences while in solitude facilitates creative thinking. Freedom is often considered a prerequisite for creative activity. To the extent, then, that solitude affords freedom of thinking it should also facilitate creativity. Csikszentmihalyi has found that adolescents who cannot tolerate being alone often fail to develop their creative talents because such development usually relies on solitary activity such as practicing one's musical instrument or writing poetry in one's journal.[47] Creativity consists of generating new useful ideas with impact by forming new associations—combinations between previously unrelated ideas. Long and Averill,[48] after adopting Schutz's analysis of multiple realities perspective, argued that cognitive characteristics associated with solitude (for example, freedom) offer opportunities for transition from the social "world of work" to the potentially creative world of "phantasy" and/or scientific theorizing. Imaginative involvement in multiple realities potentially implies the reconstitution of cognitive structures imposed by the often highly structured environments and functions of the leaders.

Solitude could increase the level of external stimulation and, at this state, according to Suedfeld and associates, the person may begin (sensing) internal stimuli such as physical sensation, shifting emotions, daydreams, and distorted thoughts.[49] Storr maintains that "learning, thinking, innovation and being in

45 Daft, R.L., & Lengel, R.H. (1998). *Fusion Leadership: Unlocking the subtle forces that change people and organizations*. San Francisco, CA: Berrett-Koehler Publishers.
46 Bruch, H., & Ghoshal, S. (2004). *A Bias for Action*. San Francisco, CA: Harvard Business School Press.
47 Csikszentmilhaly, M. (1996). *Creativity, Flow and the Psychology of Discovery and Invention*. New York: Harper Collins.
48 Long, C., & Averill, J. (2003). Solitude: an exploration of benefits of being alone. *Journal of the Theory of Social Behavior*, 33(1), 21–44.
49 Suedfeld, P. (1982). Aloneness as a healing experience. In L.A. Peplau and D. Perlman (Eds), *Loneliness: A sourcebook of current theory, research and therapy* (pp. 54–67). New York: Wiley & Sons.

contact with one's own world of imagination are all facilitated by solitude."[50] Specifically, he believes that prayer and meditation, as practices of solitude state, facilitate integration by allowing time for previously unrelated thoughts and feelings to interact: "Being able to get in touch with one's deepest thoughts and feelings, and providing time for them to regroup themselves into new formations and combinations, are important aspects of the creative processes." Maslow[51] directly links creativity to solitude by stating that the ability to become "lost in the present" seems to be a sine qua non for creativity—in whatever field as it has something to do with this "ability to become timeless, selfless, outside of space, of society, of history."

Moreover, solitude reinforces the leader's creative thinking in indirect ways. As already reported, solitude can facilitate the self-transformation, envisioning, and willpower of a leader. By self-transformation we mean that they can view things through different glasses and thus discover new dimensions, ideas, and solutions. A leader's vision, according to Senge, can strengthen his creative tension to discover new and probably revolutionary ways to eliminate the gap between the current and the desired reality.[52] A number of researchers sustain that the discovery of innovative and creative ideas comes from the internal motivation for achievement.

A second positive effect of solitude is the contribution of inner peace and inner security to the better utilization of the cognitive skills of a leader. Inner peace as a psychological state of solitude allows the leader, free of noises and with a most clear-cool thought, to analyze and understand various pieces of information and the relations between these, to wonder and to challenge the correctness of his assumptions and his beliefs, to see his self as an actor and observer simultaneously, and thus to judge more objectively, calmly, and correctly. One of the most important findings resulting from the research conducted by Fielder and his associates[53] is that, under low stress, intelligence is positively correlated and experience negatively correlated with performance.

Manz and Neck propose the concept of "self-leadership of thought" and propose a self-leadership procedure for establishing constructive thought

---

50 Storr, A. (1988). *Solitude. A return to the self.* New York: Free Press, p. 29.
51 Maslow, A.H. (1970). *Motivation and Personality* (2nd edn). New York: Harper & Row.
52 Senge, P. (1990). *The Fifth Discipline.* New York: Double Day/Currency.
53 Heifetz, R., & Linsky, M. (2002). A survival guide for leaders. *Harvard Business Review*, 65–74; Fiedler, F.E. & Garcia, J.E. (1987). *New approaches to effective leadership.* Wiley & Sons: New York.

patterns.[54] Solitude can care "the analysis and management of: 1) belief and assumptions, 2) internal dialogues (self-talk) and 3) mental images which the authors consider as 'primary vehicles' for establishing and maintaining constructive desirable thought patterns."

Third, in solitude, a leader can keep a distance from the reality that he experiences and take the position of the observer, he can see things from far and high and so have a balcony or helicopter view or a big picture of something which can help him in his thinking and judgment. Heifetz & Linsky call this skill "getting off the dance floor and going to the balcony." Great athletes must simultaneously play the game and observe it as a whole. They argue that leaders have to be both an observer and participant at the same time, having to move back and forth from the balcony to the dance floor, over and over again throughout, days, weeks, months, and years. As an example, the authors propose a simple technique for enhancing this ability of the leader. They suggest that "during a meeting, a leader, by pushing his chair a few inches away from the table after he speaks, could have the literal as well as metaphorical distance he needs to become an observer."[55]

Finally, we could assume that the freedom, social detachment, and inner security experienced by a leader in a state of solitude may help him or her to make tough decisions. Leaders often have to take tough unambiguous decisions whether they refer to people, to strategic choices, or to circumstances of high risk and uncertainty. Freedom, social detachment, and inner peace experienced by a leader in state of solitude help him to control his sense of anxiety and make it easier for him to make tough decisions which are probably unpleasant to people by touching "sacred cows," undiscussable taboos, or the zone of comfort witnessed by people within their status quo. Such decisions are also facilitated by the fact that, in a state of solitude, one can support such decisions by using his "inner voice," his deeper beliefs and a stronger feeling of self-confidence and "locus of control." Besides, solitude makes it easier for the leader to judge information efficiently, to think intuitively, and to use his gut feelings which contribute considerably to making strategic choices for the future.

---

54 Manz, C.C., & Neck, C.P. (1999). *Mastering Self-leadership: Empowering yourself for personal excellence* (2nd edn). Upper Saddle River, NJ: Prentice Hall.
55 Heifetz, R.A., & Linsky, M. (June, 2002). A survival guide for leaders. *Harvard Business Review*, 1–11.

Solitude Enables Cognitive Resilience

The benefits of inner peace and inner security in solitude are directly related to cognitive resilience. Cognitive resilience describes the capacity to overcome the negative effect of setbacks and associates stress with cognitive function. Researchers have provided evidence that the stress effects on human performance, in general, follow an inverted U curve, which means that up to a specific point the impact is positive (for example, it stimulates creativity, motivation for goal achievement) and after that it turns to negative (for example, fatigue, depression, anxiety). Cognitive resilience is a critical capability for executive leaders under a condition of high job demands, which are a potential source and determinant of executives' mental strain, anxiety, and stress as well as physical health. According to the empirical evidence of much research, stress negatively affects the cognitive function of attention, memory, and judgment. At the executive level, when job demands, as a stress source, become extremely high, executives have the tendency to engage in simplified search, analysis, and decision making—giving way to outright decision desperation.

The ability to experience solitude episodes when necessary could enhance the cognitive resilience of leaders, by three ways at least. Firstly, the immediate liberation from any external pressures weakens the potential source of stress. Secondly, the individual is able to prioritize and allocate their limited cognitive resources more effectively, thus resulting in focused attention, sharpness, and astuteness, which in turn enables them to gain control over situations. Thirdly, the liberation from external pressures (and the consequent availability of time) allows the leader to reflect on past experiences, on successes and failures, to make the most out of them and deal with the causes of stress and enhance cognitive resilience.

Solitude as an Enabler of Ethical Leadership

Another product or competence derived from solitude is that it sets the ground for initiation reflection upon our individual actions and behaviors and also on patterns of social interactions. When entering the solitude state voluntarily, the external constraints, boundaries, and demands are forced apart and inevitably we are left with our authentic self and the ensuing judgments of our own morality. In other words, solitude enables a physical, cognitive, and emotional detachment from stimuli, which allows the leader to continue their inner journey without getting sidetracked into the pains and pleasures along the way. In that way, solitude leads to some form of liberation from the emotions that accompany objects and people and from others' expectations from us. Storr[56] has suggested that by extracting us from our customary social and physical contexts, or at least altering our experience of them, solitude can remove those people and objects that define and confirm executives' closest identities and facilitate reflection and the activation of secondary, yet equally important identities.

Apart from the instant calmness and equanimity, it is theorized that such processes further facilitate the realization that our self-concept is comprised of more than one important identity, namely an executive as a citizen, moral person, and ethical role model. This awareness results in grasping the holism of our social presence and the impact of our place in the organization and society in general, which in turn enables a broader ethical perspective in executive decision making and action. In ignorance of our multiple identities, the attention is more likely focused on satisfying a narrow span of interests, which in most cases would not transcend the boundaries of the organization.

Avolio and associates clearly propose that authentic leaders are characterized by three key moral elements: moral capacity, moral efficacy, and moral courage to deal with potential moral dilemmas and challenges.[57] Self-regulation focuses on the wilful intentional acts in which people engage to increase efficacy-related behaviors. Authentic leaders harmonize the social and private aspects of self, and align themselves with the person they ideally want to be—their ideal self, dreams, and aspirations. Self-regulation also involves processes such as altering one's own behavior, resisting temptation, and so on, which indicate that the self is taking action to enhance moral capacity; it selects a morally superior response from numerous options, filters irrelevant information, and is responsible for response selection and enactment.

Self-regulation is thus the process through which authentically ethical leadership behavior that is related to the increase of moral efficacy and capacity emerges, via the alignment of the inner self, schemas, values, emotions, and cognitions with the publically adopted behaviors and actions. As an enhancer of moral courage via self-regulatory processes, solitude helps leaders manage their painful emotions and inner tensions which may decrease their energy, increase their focus and commitment to vision and goals, facilitate the alignment of action with personal values, and identify a clear vision and goals.

---

56 Storr, A. (1988). *Solitude. A return to the self.* New York: Free Press.
57 Avolio, B.J., Gardner, W.L., Waluabwa, F.O., Luthans, F., & May, D.R. (2004). Unlocking the mask: A look at the process by which authentic leaders impact follower attitudes and behaviors. *The Leadership Quarterly*, 15(6), 801–823.

Bruch and Ghoshal[58] argue that effective leaders know exactly how to process their painful emotions and inner tensions and conflicts. Most of the strategies they highlight include a process of self-reflection and a state of solitude. So, in a state of solitude, leaders are able to distance themselves and appreciate prior wins, reflect on overcome obstacles and quietly go through the failures; by doing this, their self-confidence, sense of competence and inner moral courage are reinforced.

Acting as a moral manager involves grappling not only effectively but ethically with complexity. We describe how more complex dynamics activated via solitude enhance an executive's capacity for the kind of cognitive work that effectively navigates the immense complexity of information and demands involved in executive decision making with ethics. Balancing business performance and ethics, shareholders' profits and other stakeholders' interests, and short-term profitability goals and long-term sustainability demands, are some examples. That is, balancing strategy and ethics allows an executive to positively and convincingly impact perceptions that he or she is able to act as a moral manager and this includes others' understanding that this concern for ethical management is truly authentic.

The process we describe here is guided by complex processes of meta-cognition—the systematic and in-depth examination of one's own cognitive processes and the ability for re-wiring or redirecting one's cognitive effort accordingly. We suggest that this sort of meta-cognitive processes is enabling the integration between an executive's own moral awareness (moral person) with executive action as a moral manager and that this kind of integration is entirely difficult outside spaces for reflection and mental disconnection from social and time pressures, and pressures from structured processes of power that are de facto part of today's executive role context. This sort of activation occurs when it is very difficult to distinguish the inner from the outer focus of the experience of solitude, and this is of vital importance for executive-level ethical leadership. It is required when an executive action is, at the same time, a meeting between person and role (a very personal way in which an executive chooses to confront and interpret morality and ethics including the appreciation of the subjectivity involved in any personal understanding of an issue), and an impersonal response to the executive role, requiring the effective and efficient resolution of pressing, specific problems and complex issues. Although it has been theorized by literature that the sort of integration implied here emanates from an executive's self system, we suggest that the ability to activate solitude

---

58 Bruch, H., & Ghoshal, S. (2004). *A Bias for Action*. San Francisco, CA: Harvard Business School Press.

also enables the integration between the person and manager moral awareness and concern, at least in executive leadership where the level of complexity of the issues to be dealt with is particularly high.

To summarize, solitude utilized to enhance the executive's ability to act as a moral manager and effectively grapple complexity and ethics involves effectively balancing conflicting stakeholder interests. Moreover, solitude can give the executive the opportunity to broaden their focus from just looking at performance variables (for example, only the bottom line) to a more general picture of the organization, and also allows the time and perspective to set short-term and long-term goals.

Solitude and Connection with Others

Empathy is a main dimension of emotional intelligence and a basic leadership competence. Empathy refers to the understanding and consideration of the other party's situation, feelings, and perspectives. Empathy enables the individual to take another individual's position and to experience the situation from that individual's circumstances and point of view. Koch[59] stressed that the state of solitude should not be mistakenly interpreted as lack of reaching outward to imaginary or projected communication with others. Nisenbaum conducted an extensive review of popular songs, novels, and dictionary definitions and concluded that solitude often involves feelings of connection with other people.[60] Indeed, scientifically obtained empirical evidence indicates that solitude contributes to an individual's ability to empathize with others by facilitating the development of intimacy, especially toward those who are important to this individual.[61] In the case of leadership, the followers of the leader assume the role of the important ones. Modell suggested that the person in solitude can be sustained by the projected presence of a real or imagined person.[62] For example, feeling isolated from those we care about tends to increase our desire to be close to them. The leader must feel close to her immediate associates, but also to the rest of the people under her leadership (distance leadership) in terms of understanding their feelings, fears, and hopes, but also in terms of having feelings of loving affection toward them.

---

59 Koch, P. (1994). *Solitude. A philosophical encounter*. La Salle, IL: Open Court.
60 Nisenbaum, S. (1984). Ways of being alone in the world. *American Behavioral Scientist*, 27(6), 785–800.
61 Long, C., & Averill, J. (2003). Solitude: an exploration of benefits of being alone. *Journal of the Theory of Social Behavior*, 33(1), 21–44.
62 Modell, A. (1993). *The Private Self*. Cambridge, MA: Harvard UP.

However, in the environment where leadership is normally exercised (for example, the work organization) the constant pressure to achieve results as well as the natural or hierarchical distance render the attainment of intimacy very difficult. Therefore, solitude can operate in a compensatory way by generating the required intimacy to feed the process of empathetic feelings of the leader for his associates and followers

The Practice of Solitude

A qualitative study employing 20 upper-level leaders and a quantitative in the middle and upper level has been conducted which provides a useful insight into the practice of solitude.[63] It is interesting to present here the results that concern the frequency of solitude episodes, the emotions, and their duration, along with the motives and the benefits of the participants involved.

The results of the quantitative research reveal that 77 percent of the participants responded that they systematically aim to be in a state of solitude, as indicated by their answer "many times," while another 11 percent responded "few times," which signifies that 88 percent of the leaders who participated in the study consciously and actively seek for solitary time. As follows, only the remaining participants, namely 12 percent, state that they do not engage in solitude very often.

The responses to the question investigating the context and environment in which leaders prefer to engage in solitude were: travelling in remote places, exercising, walking, staying home, or visiting nature reserves. Other situations appearing further down the list were: going to an organized retreat, travel time, isolating one's self in the office, going to the theater, and watching a movie.

The leaders were also asked about the reasons that usually make them want to spend some time alone. The responses here were twofold. On one hand, they resort to solitude because of negative pressures or a repelling and unbearable work environment (stress, physical and mental fatigue, lack of time, bad temper). On the other hand, they seem to acknowledge that solitude offers a series of benefits, among which are inner peace, sense of freedom, inner security, reflection, self-determination, and intimacy. Table 6.3 provides a detailed presentation of these benefits.

---

63 Kardasi, O. (2014). Solitude as a leadership meta-competence. Unpublished doctoral dissertation, Athens University of Economics and Business, Athens: Greece.

Table 6.3   The main benefits of solitude

To what degree do you feel the following?	A great deal/much/somewhat
I have the opportunity to deepen my thinking and calm down	90%
I reflect on my actions	81%
I feel comfortable to make decisions	79%
I feel calmed and focused on the things I care about	79%
I come up with innovative ideas and solutions	76%
I feel free to engage in activities that make me relax	71%
My anxiety is reduced	70%
I think positively of the others	70%
I feel confident of myself	69%
I see things from different perspectives	62%
I let go of thoughts and relax	61%
I step back from everyday problems and my mind clears	57%
I have positive feelings for the others	50%
I feel calmness and serenity without thinking anything	46%
My confidence recovers	41%

The survey participants were further asked, in the form of an open question, about the emotions that they experience before, during, and after they engage in solitude episodes. They eagerly expressed a variety and multitude of emotions which can be found in Table 6.4.

Similar eagerness was observed when leaders were asked to mention the reasons that were most likely to make them want to spend time alone. A participant stated that "over-thinking about work and related problems creates the need for discharge, expanding one's horizons and recovering." Another participant characteristically attested that "the constant need for socialization, as manifest in the long hours spent on meetings, conferences, in front of a computer screen, or talking on the phone, has left no time for contemplation—preferably alone." In the same vein, another participant, underlining the need not to be carried away by the incessant flow of events, graphically says, "I need to disconnect myself from the everyday problems that drag me down and see the situation from a distance, if I want to make things better. Given that I do not possess any psychic abilities, in order to manage the vast amount of information, I have to detach and look at things from my point of view and not through the eyes of others. Oftentimes, routine traps you in and without even realizing, you end up reacting mechanically to situations instead of creatively and reflectively attempting to resolve them."

In the quantitative study, leaders were also asked which events triggered the need for resorting to solitude. From the responses, which are summarized in Table 6.5, we can decipher that solitude functions as an important enabler for a number of leadership aspects, such as decision making and self-management.

Furthermore, the participants were referred to specific decisions that were made after they spent creative time alone. So, for example, leaders mentioned that they made up their mind concerning the rearranging of a dealer's network, the expansion into a new sector, changing job, the investment on innovation and creativity, a major acquisition, and the restructuring of a company.

Table 6.4   Emotions that arise before, during and after the solitude episodes

Before solitude	During solitude	After solitude
Self-examination	Relief	Re-approaching problems
Agony	Review things	Calmness
Anxiety	Organizing thinking	Crystallization of thinking
Physical fatigue	Creativity	Cheer
Mental fatigue	Rejoicing	Joy of achievement
Moodiness	Mindfulness	Satisfaction
The peak moment of creative innovation	Calmness	Pleasure
Distancing	Mental stimulation	Shielding
Relaxation	Vigilance	Serenity
Clarity of mind	Mental tension	Self-control

Table 6.5   Events that trigger the solitude episodes

To what degree do the following events make you want spend time alone?	A great deal/much/ somewhat
Problem solutions	86%
Matters concerning the people of the company or my team	80%
Changes/improvements in my company or team	78%
Personal dilemmas	73%
The long-term objectives of my company or team	72%
My future	72%
The short-term objectives of my company or my team	71%
My personal values	71%
My career	70%
Innovations	69%
The vision of my company	69%
Listening my inner voice	67%
Crucial decisions for the organization or team	65%
My personal vision	63%
The values of my company or team	62%
Business strategy issues	59%
Reflecting on past experiences	56%
Who am I and where I want to go	53%
My ideal self	52%

Solitude as a Leadership Meta-Competence

The thesis of the present work is that solitude is a meta-competence for leadership. However, solitude fulfils its role as leadership meta-competence successfully only when the leader desires and seeks it and is able to experience it constructively. Only in this way can the leader benefit from its positive influence on the emotional and cognitive processes that facilitate effective leadership. Long and associates[64] conclude that, in order to benefit from solitude, the individual must be able to draw on inner resources to find meaning in situations in which external support is lacking. It appears that there is a rather fine line that separates solitude from loneliness. Solitude is and remains a beneficial state to the extent

---

64 Long, C., Seburn, M., Averill, J., & T. More. (2003). Solitude experiences: Varieties, settings and individual differences. *Personality and Social Psychology Bulletin*, 29(5), 578–583.

that the individual desires and chooses to enter it voluntarily and selectively (that is, only in certain occasions and for specific reasons). Otherwise, the danger is that the state in which the individual enters is not solitude, but loneliness, the consequences of which, as seen, are not positive. It appears that solitude is an "ecological niche" that offers both opportunities and dangers hence, whether the former will be avoided, or vice versa, depends on the abilities of the person.[65] Individuals differ in their desire and preference for solitude.[66] In addition, the need to enter into the state of solitude depends on situational contingencies (for example, frequency of encountering difficult situations, and so on). Therefore the competence of solitude includes the ability of the individual to understand when there is a need for solitude and to engage in the state in the appropriate degree.

Concluding Thoughts

In addition, considering the points made previously along with some early empirical results, the ability of the leader to experience solitude constructively may be related to enduring personality traits such as extroversion (which encompasses sociability and the ability to experience positive emotions) and agreeableness (which encompasses altruism and sensitivity to the needs of others). Moreover, even when the agent enters solitude consciously and voluntarily, it can still harmoniously coexist and even reinforce the aforementioned traits, supporting the notion of the leadership complexity paradox, as proposed by Quinn and associates.[67] For example, when we have spent some time alone and away from loved ones, our craving to meet and communicate with them is magnified.

When examining the roots of solitude, there seems to be an agreement that it is a competence that can be learnt and acquired at an early age. For example, the mother can be largely responsible for providing a secure environment in which the child can experience "being alone in the presence of the mother."[68] However, the ability to achieve solitude can be cultivated in adult life as well by means of methods and techniques such as mediation, dissociation, retreat, and personal exercise.

---

65 Larson R., & Lee, M. (1996). The capacity to be alone as a stress buffer. *Journal of Social Psychology*, 136(1), 5–16

66 Burger J.M. (1995). Individual differences in preference of solitude. *Journal of Research in Personality*, 29(1), 85–108.

67 Quinn, R.E., Spreitzer, G.M., & Brown, M.V. (2000). Changing others through changing ourselves. *Journal of Management Inquiry*, 9(2), 147–164.

68 Storr A. (1988). *Solitude. A return to the self.* New York: Free Press.

Chapter 7

The Issue of Trust

Introduction

Numerous studies from diverse scientific fields, such as sociology, psychology, economics, and management, attest that trust is the cornerstone for qualitative and efficient relations between individuals, teams, and organizations. Indeed, if we think for a moment the negative feelings resulting from the lack of trust in any kind of social relationship—such as, for example, between husband and wife, parents and children, colleagues, employers and employees, suppliers and customers, doctors and patients—we can easily understand the tremendous importance that trust entails in every aspect of our lives. Apart from that, for an organization or a firm, trust can also serve as competitive advantage since it constitutes the base for the social capital, organizational commitment, motivation, and engagement of the employees, the acquisition and maintenance of loyal customers, investors, suppliers, and other partners. When it comes to society, it is at the source of its reputation.

As follows, the absence of trust begets uncertainty, insecurity and fear, and problematic communication; people tend to keep secrets from each other, they avoid expressing ideas, opinions, and feelings, they tend to protect themselves rather than cooperate, and they recur to bureaucracy to cover their "back." When it comes to leadership, as a reciprocal and influential process between those who aspire to lead and those who choose to follow, trust is a paramount prerequisite.

Although it is hardly doubtful or ambiguous that trust is the lifeblood of any relationship, the past decades abound with critical incidents of trust erosion in leadership, societies, institutions, and the list goes on. In a recent study[1] it was revealed that people in China do not trust the official sources of information, namely newspapers or television, but instead they are more ready

---

1   Chen, X., & Shi, T. (2001). Media effects on political confidence and trust in the People's Republic of China in the post-Tiananmen period. *East Asia*, 19(3), 84–118

to believe anonymous online bloggers. Moreover, the numerous scandals (political or ethical), bankruptcies, and the financial crisis augment the negative consequences of distrust as evident in the feeling expressed by a large part of the workforce that their psychological contracts have been violated, while at the same time many investors feel betrayed, and many customers become suspicious and thus disloyal.

In this chapter, having at our disposal the rich but somehow complicated available bibliography on trust, we will attempt to elucidate the meaning and the benefits of this vital attribute. Relying on the existing theories, we approach trust from various conceptual levels such as the individual, team, and organizational, and we further discuss the personal traits, behaviors, and practices of leaders that are likely to enhance their own trustworthiness as well as trust placed in the team and the organization.

The Meaning of Trust

The most accepted definitions from the plethora being proposed in the relevant literature are the ones offered by Mayer et al.[2] and Rousseau et al.[3] The first scholars define trust as: "the willingness of a party to be vulnerable to the actions of another party based on expectation that the other will perform a particular action important to the trustor, irrespective of the ability to monitor or control that other party."[4] Similarly, Rousseau and colleagues describe trust as "a psychological state comprising the intention to accept vulnerability based upon positive expectations of the intentions or behaviour of another." Both definitions include an expectation that another party will perform a particular action within the context of a relationship, while at the same time trust is associated with certain uncertainty and risk.

Another line of research places the emphasis on the specific characteristics of the trustees such as ability, benevolence, and integrity, terms to which we shall refer in the following pages. Moreover, despite the importance of trust across multiple levels in organizations, the majority of studies have focused on the individual level. In an attempt to fill that gap, Fulmer and Gelfand in an

---

2   Mayer, R.C., Davis, J.H., & Schoorman, F.D. (1995). An integrative model of organizational trust. *Academy of Management Review*, 20(3), 709–734.

3   Rousseau, D.M., Sitkin, S.B., Burt, R.S., & Camerer, C. (1998). Not so different after all: A cross-discipline view of trust. *Academy of Management Review*, 23(3), 393–404.

4   Mayer, R.C., Davis, J.H., & Schoorman, F.D. (1995). An integrative model of organizational trust. *Academy of Management Review*, 20(3), 709–734.

extensive and exemplary research paper, provide a systematic review of trust research across levels and across referents.[5] In this review, the authors adopt a multi-level analysis that includes interpersonal, team, and organization at the individual, team, and organizational levels. The interpersonal referent refers to the specific other such as the leader or the co-workers, the team referent refers to trust in the team, and the organization referent refers to the trust in an entity such as an organization.

Using this distinction and valuing the previous definitions we obtain a specific definition of trust across levels and referents: We define trust in an interpersonal referent at the individual level, as a psychological state that comprises the willingness to accept vulnerability based on positive expectations of a specific other or others; trust in an interpersonal referent at the team level as a shared psychological state among team members that comprises the willingness to accept vulnerability based on positive expectations of a specific other or others; and trust in an interpersonal referent at the organizational level as a shared psychological state among organizational members that comprises the willingness to accept vulnerability based on positive expectations of a specific other and others. Likewise, trust in an organization at the individual level is defined as a psychological state that comprises the willingness to accept vulnerability based on positive expectations of an organization, and trust in an organization at the organizational level as "a shared psychological state among organization's members that comprises willingness to accept vulnerability based on positive expectations of an organization."[6]

The Benefits of Trust

Until today, numerous papers and studies have been published that corroborate the positive attributes and attitudes of trust which are either directly or indirectly related to the performance of individuals, teams, and organizations. In addition, examining the relative literature, we can determine a series of arguments and benefits which, in spite of being sporadically mentioned, have not become the focus of academic research. Therefore, the next few chapters are devoted to presenting the benefits of trust which, for the sake of understanding, are categorized in three distinct levels, namely the individual, the team, and the organization.

---

5   Fulmer, C.A., & Gelfand, M.J. (2012). At what level (and in whom) we trust: Trust across multiple organizational levels. *Journal of Management*, 38, 1167–1230.
6   Brower, H., Schoorman, D., & Hoon Tan, H. (2000). A model of relational leadership: The integration of trust and leader-member exchange. *Leadership Quarterly*, 11(2), 227–250.

Table 7.1   The benefits of trust for leaders

- Followers' satisfaction and commitment to leader.
- Climate of open communication, sense of freedom to express opinions, dissent, accurate information, ideas, suggestions, feeling which enhances the creativity, innovativeness and proactiveness of decision making and problem solving.
- Followers' engagement, organizational citizen behavior, initiatives, willingness to go the extra mile.
- Leaders receive accurate and constructive positive and negative feedback.
- Followers' consensus, acceptance, and support of changes initiated by the leaders.
- Team safety, potency, and performance.

1. THE BENEFIT OF TRUST TO THE LEADER (INDIVIDUAL LEVEL)

In this first level of analysis, we examine how leaders can gain the trust of their followers. If we contemplated the role of leadership, perhaps the first characteristic that would pop out is that a leader exercises influence over other people. The way the influence is actualized varies substantially, but the common denominator might be the formulation and communication of a vision. Indeed, the leader, by putting things into perspective, becomes able to unite, direct, and develop their people to such a degree that the latter become independent, aware, empowered, and oriented toward achieving results not only for themselves, but for the team, the organization, and the greater community. Needless to say, hardly anyone is willing to take a risk of following someone, accepting and believing their vision and making any sort of effort unless they trust that the leader is integral, fair, and competent enough to lead them there. The saying that goes, "Who you are speaks so loudly I can hardly hear what you say," aptly expresses the importance of trustworthiness in the relation the leaders maintain with the followers. No one believes the message unless he trusts the emitter. Therefore, trust in the leader is a paramount prerequisite of effective leadership and followership.[7]

Table 7.1 summarizes some of the findings that have been empirically found to result from trust. Thus, when there has been established trust between a leader and followers, the latter get feelings of satisfaction from themselves and from the job, they support the leader even in the face of unfavorable outcomes, they believe in the information provided by the leader, they accept the leader's decisions and goals, they develop a sense of ownership and become more

---

7   Colquitt, J.A., Scott, B.A., & LePine, J.A. (2007). Trust, trustworthiness, and trust propensity: A meta-analytic test of their unique relationships with risk taking and job performance. *Journal of Applied Psychology*, 92(4), 909–927.

accountable, responsible, and committed to the goal execution and attainment. Trust in leaders reduces the followers' uncertainty in their work since their attention is focused on the job and they are not distracted by unnecessary worry and anxiety.[8]

Furthermore, research strongly suggests that by trusting the leader, the followers are more willing to go above and beyond required tasks, to go the "extra mile." Moreover, trust in the leader is positively related to the followers' organizational citizen behavior, which is described as any behavior beneficial to the team and the organization that is not prescribed by the bureaucracy of job descriptions. For example, such behavior could be extra working hours, chatting with a co-worker who is distraught over a personal problem, and coaching and mentoring a new employee in the norms and the culture of the organization.[9]

Another important benefit of trusting the leader is the establishment of a climate that promotes open communication. This further implies that followers are not afraid to speak up about what they see, know, feel, understand, and believe; in other words it reduces the possibility of employees remaining silent. Employee silence refers to situations where employees withhold information that might be useful to the organization. Apparently, if such a climate of silence sets in, the results can be catastrophic for the proactive resolution of problems, creativity, adaptability, continuous improvement, innovativeness, and consensus. In addition, it causes dissatisfaction and frustration to the employees, a decrease in the level of commitment to the leaders and the organization, and increases their intention to quit. Instead, when people trust their leader, they are unafraid to speak up, which in turn increases the amount of information, ideas, and potential solutions for problems that are brought to the leader's attention; as a result, the creativity of both, that is, the trustor and the trustee, is likely to flourish.

However, it would be an omission not to mention that, apart from the benefits of trusting the leader for the followers, it is also the leader that enjoys a series of benefits. So, when people trust the leader and feel free to express themselves, the former can obtain more accurate and constructive— positive or negative—feedback, which is an indispensable element for accurate

8   Burke, C., Sims, D., Lazzra, E., and Salas, E. (2007). Trust in leadership: A multilevel review and integration. *Leadership Quarterly*, 18(6), 606–632.
9   Coyle-Shapiro, J. (2002). A psychological contract perspective on organizational citizenship behavior. *Journal of Organizational Behavior*, 23(8), 927–946.

self-evaluation, self-awareness, and self-development.[10] On top of that, the followers' trust makes the leaders clarify and believe more in the reason and legitimacy of the organizational change that they initiate. Thus, when the leader is strongly confident in the change, and followers trust them, the barriers toward change seem to fall; as a result, the levels of followers' involvement and exercise of effort in order to materialize the change plans increase, which in turn positively affects the likelihood of success.

2. THE BENEFITS OF TRUST AMONG TEAM MEMBERS (TEAM LEVEL)

Research on trust among team members reveals that it affects team performance and the sense of psychological safety. When team members trust each other, on one hand we observe decreased levels of suspicion, confrontation, and conflicts and, on the other, increased levels of a team's satisfaction, open communication, mutual understanding, and respect for diversity. Ultimately, team trust results in efficient and effective cooperation and achievement of synergies.

Table 7.2 indicates team learning as another important benefit resulting from the establishment of trust among team members. So, with trust, the members of a team do not avoid risks but are willing to share and combine their knowledge, experiences, and ideas in order to continually improve the team's function, efficiency, effectiveness, and innovation. In addition, trust makes the conditions suitable for constructive feedback and, hence, team members can pursue learning opportunities and improve their competencies, skills, and decision making. As a result, the possibilities for groupthink to occur are low, since the phenomenon has been empirically linked to lack of trust between team members, which is further associated with pressure to conform, and unprocessed or/and undisclosed information.

Table 7.2   The benefits of trust for teams

- Psychological safety, open communication, win–win behavior, reduced confrontation and conflicts.
- Mutual understanding, respect of diversity.
- Knowledge sharing and team learning.
- Enhance the team capacity for consensus.

---

10 Gao, L., Janssen, O., & Shi, K. (2011). Leader trust and employee voice: The moderating role of empowering leader behaviors. *Leadership Quarterly*, 22, 787–798.

A final point to be made regarding the positive effects of trust among team members lies in the resultant potency of achieving consent instead of compromising. Consent presupposes the members' predisposition to persuade and be persuaded, the free expression of their arguments and the challenging of them, mutual understanding, and everyone's participation in the dialogue, decision-making, or problem-solving processes. As follows, team members develop a sense of ownership in the decision-making or problem-solving, a sense of responsibility for the execution of the plan, and a sense of engagement in the results.

3. THE BENEFITS OF TRUST TO THE ORGANIZATION (ORGANIZATIONAL LEVEL)

The literature on organizational trust takes various perspectives as it includes the trust of the employees toward the organization and vice versa, the interorganizational trust, which refers to trust between two organizations, and the trust developed between the organization and its customers. To begin with, organizations with high levels of cultural trust tend to produce quality products and services because they tend to attract a highly skilled and motivated workforce. Those employees feeling secure and not threatened by possible psychological contract violations are more committed to the organization, and as a consequence exhibit a strong intention to stay in the organization, are more engaged to work harder, embrace the organization's vision, values, and mission, and in general, they demonstrate a higher organizational citizen behavior (see Table 7.3 overleaf).

Secondly, an organizational trust climate facilitates top-down and upward communication, reduces the likelihood of organizational silence, amplifies the employees' voice, and, all of the above, in turn, reinforce the proactiveness of problem solving, effective decision making, organizational learning, continuous improvement, creativity, and innovativeness. Third, trust as an organizational trait contributes positively in cross-functional communication and knowledge sharing, transforming the organization into a boundaryless one.

On the contrary, when people don't trust the organization, the communication tends to be formalized, obeying rules and regulations becomes a priority, decision making strictly follows the chain of command and, as a result, the workforce is not given the discretion to deal with problems on its own, and people do not feel relaxed and free to express their full potential. Similarly, when the organization does not trust its people, it encourages centralization, formalization, and sets off a control mechanism thus increasing bureaucracy, which in turn obstructs any initiative, adaptability, and flexibility.

Table 7.3   The benefits of trust for the organization

- Enhance the positive organization climate.
- Commitment to organization and the intention to stay.
- Enhance employee's voice, organizational creativity, innovativeness, proactiveness, and adaptability.
- Better cross-functional cooperation and knowledge sharing, boundaryless organization.
- Less bureaucracy and control mechanisms.
- Loyal customer, shareholders, suppliers, and other stakeholders.
- Lower transaction costs, and win–win behavior with stakeholders.
- Constructive feedback, information, opinions, suggestions, ideas from stakeholders.

When examining organizational trust from the customers' point of view, empirical findings suggest that trust is key to guaranteeing the success of business relationships. Especially for service businesses, which are characterized by high degrees of risk, establishing and maintaining trust becomes vital. According to Ken Ferguson, Banking Association Chairman, "more than half of bank customers believe that having a relationship of trust with their financial institution is more important than getting the best value for money".[11] Obviously, when customers trust an organization, they are more loyal, more likely to have a stronger purchase intention, higher satisfaction, and better cooperation with the organization. Particularly in our days of new digital technologies and social media expansion, the distance between customers and the organization is diminished, giving a more interactive and personified nature to this relationship. For example, customers are given the virtual space to express opinions, needs, and ideas, give recommendations and feedback on products and services, which organizations seek and welcome.

Finally, the field of interorganizational trust is the least documented, yet it is growing. It is usually defined as the extent to which members of one organization hold a collective trust orientation toward another organization.[12] It is important to avoid anthropomorphizing the organization by treating interorganizational trust as equivalent to interpersonal trust, as the dynamics are different when appreciating systems. Concerning the benefits of this type of trust, research indicates that, apart from the direct economic, such as lower transaction costs and increase in sales, there are some indirect which include greater improved knowledge transfer, sustainability in relationships (for example, between buyer and supplier) and increased strategic flexibility.

---

11 Halliburton, C., & Poenaru, A. (2010). *The Role of Trust in Consumer Relationships*. ESCP Business School.
12 Zaheer, A., McEvily, B., & Perrone, V. (1998). Does trust matter? Exploring the effects of interorganizational and interpersonal trust on performance. *Organization Science*, 9(2), 141–159.

Despite the fact that all related research indicates that trusting a leader offers positive effects, trust alone is not a panacea—meaning that it does not work positively for all followers or under all circumstances. A recent study carried out by Zhang and Jia[13] indicates that, under certain conditions, trust may have a negative influence on the follower's performance. The authors define two parameters of trust: the cognitive trust that arises from a trustor's objective assessment of key characteristics possessed by the leader such as ability, competence, integrity, and reliability and the affective trust which is based on the emotional bond resulting from the trustor's realization that the trustee genuinely cares about the trustor and acts with the other party's welfare in mind. According to the authors' arguments, the cognitive trust in the leader can have a negative effect on the followers' performance because it may lead to over-dependence or over-reliability on the leader's face, which can elicit a free-riding or social loafing tendency on behalf of the follower, especially when the size of the team is relatively large. Therefore, in order to eliminate to a minimum the chances of allowing such negative effects to be created from the cognitive trust on followers' performance, the leaders need to specifically set each follower's job role and profile, to set specific goals for each separate group, to punish free-riding behavior, to encourage followers to accept personal responsibility, and to take initiative rather than over-relying on the ability of the leader in accomplishing the task himself.

Trust Building: The Main Work of the Leader

In the preceding chapter, it was overtly expressed that one of the leaders' primary roles is naturally associated with establishing and maintaining trust. Here, in this first part we elaborate further on this argument and then go on to explain the processes through which the leader can actually function as a trust builder. For the first issue, assuming that the relationship between leaders and followers implies influence and power, the responsibility of earning trust lies at the stronger part of the dyad, that is, the leader. So, the latter is responsible for gaining the trust of the important "others," namely the followers, management, and external partners. It is worth mentioning that the trust of followers should be earned both from an individual point of view but also as members of the team. In other words, the followers should trust the leader as a person and as part of a team capable of achieving results. Moreover, the leader is accountable for establishing trust among the members of his or her team and the rest of the

---

13 Zhang, Z., & Jia, M. (2009). When does trust influence cooperation effects in public-private partnerships? *SAM Advanced Management Journal, 74*(3), 1–21.

organizational stakeholders. For this role to be successfully accomplished, the leader needs to fully understand the antecedents of trust at every level as well as the behavior and practices through which trust can be gained. Research suggests that for trust in the organizational settings to emerge, we need to pay attention firstly to leaders' personal traits and behaviors that are positively related to trustworthiness and, secondly, to the context that the leader is responsible for creating in order to facilitate trust development toward themselves, among team members, and to the organization. In the following paragraphs, drawing from the relevant bibliography, we describe some of the most important determining factors that compose the trust-building competence of the leaders.

The Origins of Trust: Integrity, Ability, and Benevolence

There seems to be an agreement among researchers that trust is dependent on three vital traits which are integrity, ability, and benevolence. It is important to note at this point that trust is not considered just the sum of these three parameters but in fact the product, meaning that if one of the three is missing, the result is null, that is, there is no trust. Another crucial point to be made is that these traits should be evident to followers. Putting it simply, it is not enough for the leader to be integral, able, and benevolent; these traits must be perceived by others through concrete choices, behavior, and actions. Based on the fact that trust does not lie in the words of the leader but in their patterns of behavior and actions, we will now elucidate each one of the three aspects that constitute trust.

1. THE INTEGRITY FACTOR

Integrity is defined as the trustor's perception that the trustee adheres to a set of morally correct principles which the trustor finds acceptable, honest, consistent, fair, accountable, predictable, and transparent. Honesty means that the leader is perceived as truthful, ethical, and principled. Fairness and justice are at the core of honesty. Specifically, leaders need to prove their justice through three dimensions. Firstly, the distributive justice, which involves the proper allocation of resources, rewards, and promotions in a consistent and fair manner. Secondly, the procedural justice, which regards the processes that lead to decision outcomes as well as policies and, third, the interactional justice which stands for the people who are being treated with respect and with whom communication is carried out with respect and dignity and without any manipulation. Fairness is also perceived when the leader considers other's viewpoints and transcends personal biases in order to explain the decision-making process, including the provision of adequate and justified feedback. A notion closely related to fairness is dignity, which entails the respect the leader pays when interacting with their people, as exemplified by their gentle manners when, for example, avoid giving bad feedback to an employee in the presence of others.

Consistency and predictability refer to perceived congruence between shared and enacted values, between promises made and promises kept, between words and actions. This literally suggests that leaders should practice what they preach. Accountability refers to the obligation that leaders are to be held responsible for their actions and they are willing to accept responsibility. In other words, the leader assumes his own share of responsibility, recognizes personal responsibility in the event of wrong decisions or low performance, and has the courage to publicly apologize. Leaders who are personally responsible for their choices and actions, and are formally held accountable for their decision-making processes, are most likely to be perceived as having a higher level of integrity.

Another dimension of leader's integrity that contributes to winning followers' trust regards the issue of value congruence. Values are defined as internalized attitudes that determine what is right and what is wrong, ethical or unethical, good or bad, important or unimportant, appropriate or inappropriate. Several authors have documented that a crucial element of interpersonal trust lies in the belief that the two parties share common values and their consequent actions are indeed guided by the morality constraints implicit by these values. Hence, to the degree where there is value congruence between leader and followers, the leader gets more chances to be viewed as trustworthy and reliable. Following this assumption, the leader, in order to be viewed as having integrity and gain the followers' trust, must on one hand, have and live by clear values and, on the other hand, be able to formulate common values with the followers. Furthermore, the leaders' values should explicitly match the organizational ones, given that the leader is expected to stand out and act as a role model for the followers. Organizational values, then, must express the choices, attitudes, behavior, and performance of the leaders' personal values. So, for example, the leader communicates and passes on the organizational values to its followers through the locus of their attention, by what they systematically monitor and control, by a system of praise, rewards, and penalties, and the articulation of stories, slogans, and symbolisms.

However, apart from the values of each organization, integrity and the resulting trust are connected to some human values regardless of organizational and/or national culture. According to Eisenbeiss, such values are: the humane orientation, which means to treat others with dignity and respect and to see them as end not as means; the justice orientation, which refers to making fair and consistent decisions and not discriminating against others; the responsibility and the sustainability orientation, which refers to the leader's long-term view on success and his concern for the welfare of society and the environment; and finally the moderation orientation which refers to temperance, humility, and balanced leader behavior.[14] Especially today, when leaders face great diversity and a multicultural context, the mutual acceptance and practice of these core values proposed by Eisenbeiss, both by leaders and by followers, forms a concrete, solid base on which trust can be built.

Besides the previous fundamental components of integrity that have become the center of attention of the related bibliography, it would be an omission not to mention the issue of transparency which accounts considerably for the leader's perceived integrity. In particular, in today's turbulent, uncertain, complex, global environment which is often characterized by prominent examples of unethical practices, transparency constitutes an important source of trust. According to *Webster's Dictionary*,[15] "transparency" is something obvious, clear, readily understandable, candid, and lucid. Transparency guarantees that all relevant information concerning a situation, decisions, actions, and outcomes is known to all interested parties. The leader is perceived as transparent when he shares relevant information with followers, is open to give and receive feedback, makes known the motives and reasoning behind difficult and challenging decisions and situations. The leader's transparency reduces the followers' uncertainty, risk taking, ambiguity, and suspicion and increases their understanding and the predictability concerning the leader's decisions and behavior, which in turn enhances their trust in the leader. The leader transparency accounts greatly for the followers' trust, particularly today when modern circumstances demand tough decisions, speed, constant changes, and ethical practices.

2. THE ABILITY FACTOR

Ability serves as the second base for building the trust of the followers. Ability is defined as that group of skills, competencies, and characteristics that enable a party to exercise influence within some specific domain. For example,

---

14 Eisenbeiss, S.A. (2011). *The Four Minimal Orientations of Ethical Leadership: Bridging Insights from Western and Eastern Moral Philosophy and the World Religions to Management Sciences.* Paper presented at the 18th International Annual Business Ethics Conference 2011, New York, USA.

15 Norman, S.M. (2010). The impact of positivity and transparency on trust in leaders and their perceived effectiveness. *The Leadership Quarterly*, 21(3), 350–364.

nobody trusts a doctor, a teacher, or a driver unless they believe that they are adequately skilled and have the necessary knowledge and expertise to efficiently carry out the indicated tasks to the service of the others. No one follows a leader voluntarily and unreservedly unless they are convinced that the leader possesses the required knowledge and skills to guide them through the materialization of a shared vision and agreed goals, the delivery of sustainable well-being, and toward a better future. If followers don't believe in their leaders' ability, they consider them unreliable, they don't accept the goals they set, and they don't give them their best. For followers to give their trust, leaders need to demonstrate functional knowledge in their field of expertise, decision-making skills such as sound judgment, rational thinking, strategic thinking, and problem-solving capacity, human skills, as well as a set of personal traits such as courage, boldness, composure, self-regulation, and emotional intelligence. Among these, research clearly indicates two that constitute critical leading competencies and are directly linked to the followers' trust.

The first of these two important competences is the leader's ability to form and communicate a compelling direction in order to ensure that employees perceive and understand their tasks and goals as clear ones, challenging ones, and consequential ones. The leader's compelling direction targets followers and energizes and motivates them to give their best in order to achieve the expected results. But, in order to ascertain the generally accepted direction, leaders need to appreciate and interpret the opportunities and constraints of the external organizational environment, and to identify the strengths and weaknesses of their people.

The second competence is the leader's ability to conceive an organizational structure that enables the attainment of the goals and vision. This means that the leaders should be able to design the work tasks appropriately, allocate the resources fairly and rationally, and ensure the appropriate number of the right people in each team. If these two competencies are missing out, the followers perceive the leader as "out of the loop," unorganized, confused, inefficient, and ineffective and, consequently, as someone who cannot be trusted.

In a difficult, competitive, dynamic, complex, turbulent, ambiguous, and uncertain landscape, leading is not an easy task. Leading is fighting. Leadership is a struggle. Therefore, the ability to lead, besides the already mentioned knowledge and skills, demands courage, self-confidence, resilience, tenacity, perseverance, and optimism to take tough decisions, challenge the status quo, take risks, face dilemmas ambivalences, and also to think big and think ahead.

Without these, no leader can ever expect to persuade followers of his or her ability to lead and fight for victory.

Drawing from the works of positive psychology and positive organizational behavior, we identified four leader's traits that reinforce the ability to lead and, consequently, are connected to followers' trust. First, both leadership and trust need hope. Hope is defined as a positive motivational state that is based on an interactively derived sense of successful a) agency (goal-directed energy) and b) pathways (planning to meet goals). Second, leadership and trust in leaders need resiliency. Resiliency means "a positive psychological capacity to rebound, to bounce back from diversity, uncertainty, conflict, failure or even positive change, progress, and increased co-responsibility."[16] Third, leadership and trust in the leader needs realistic optimism. Realistic optimism means that the leader has a positive outlook and makes positive attributions regarding events that may be perceived by less optimistic individuals as inhibiting their motivation. Optimism is the belief that there is a great chance of attaining the figures and goals of an organization despite the restrictions, hardship, and obstacles that abound. Fourth, leadership and trust in the leader requires efficacy. Efficacy means that the leader is convinced that his ability is sufficient to motivate cognitive resources or courses of action that are required for the successful execution of a specific task within a given context. These four components essentially complete the perceived ability of leaders and make their followers feel less insecure regarding the correctness and the efficiency of the leadership and thus, provide a higher level of trust.

3. THE BENEVOLENCE FACTOR

Benevolence is the perception of positive orientation in the trustee to the extent that the trustee is believed to want to do right by the trustor, regardless of egocentric profit and motif. The leaders, by exhibiting a genuinely supportive, caring and mentor–protégé behavior (demonstrated through sympathy, cooperation, and help), make the followers understand that they can rely on them. Two particular benevolent behaviors that lead followers to judge their leader as benevolent are the provision of expert coaching and the creation of a supportive context.

---

16 Luthans, F., Norman, S.M., Avolio, B.J., & Avey, J.B. (2008). The mediating role of psychological capital in the supportive organizational climate-employee performance relationship. *Journal of Organizational Behavior*, 29(2), 219–238.

Table 7.4   How leaders gain the trust of their followers

- They demonstrate integrity, transparency, justice, fairness, honesty, dignity, and morality.
- They demonstrate accountability, responsibility for their actions, and recognize their mistakes.
- They say what they mean and they mean what they say, they keep promises, practice what they preach, and they walk the talk.
- They assure the congruence of values among others, the cross-cultural, such as human orientation, justice, responsibility, and sustainability orientation and moderation orientation.
- They demonstrate ability by setting a compelling direction and creating an enabling structure.
- They express positive psychology, hope, realistic optimism, resilience. and efficacy.
- They demonstrate benevolence, willingness to do the good thing, are willing to demonstrate empathy, sympathy, to provide help, care, support, and to coach followers.

Coaching is one of the leader's main roles since it contributes to the development of an effective culture. Today's coaching is not just about task improvement and better people, it is all about having a team that is aligned to a clear strategy and embraces being held accountable to delivering on that strategy. Individual coaching, either as constructive negative feedback or as teaching and exposure to new experiences, makes followers grow mature and indicates the leader's genuine concern for their development and welfare—something that, in return, builds the followers' trust in the leader.

By creating a supportive context, the leader ensures the availability of information, resources, processes, establishment of a positive climate, and participation in problem solving and decision making; these attributes enable followers to perform their duties and achieve their goals pleasantly and efficiently. Additionally, the behavior of demonstrating individualized support becomes even more important when viewed under the trust prism. Through one-to-one interaction, the leader listens, deeply understands, and sympathizes with the followers' personal and professional problems, anxieties and fears, expectations and dilemmas, and confronts them through counselling, mentoring, encouragement, and help (see Table 7.4).

Building Trust within a Team and an Organization

Not only is the leader responsible for gaining the trust of followers and significant others, they are also responsible for building trust among team members and diffusing a climate of trust throughout the organization as a whole in such a way that trustworthiness becomes a team and organizational trait, and not just an individual trait.

Table 7.5   **How leaders build trust among team members**

- Set clear norms, procedures, and processes.
- Create a climate of open communication and mental feedback.
- Create a culture of integrity and responsibility.
- Select team members with propensity to trust and trustworthiness.
- Enhance the value congruence among team members.

Regarding trust among team members, the leader's actions focus on five basic domains (see Table 7.5). First, the leader must build a strong team culture in order to ensure the value congruence among team members. A team culture that ensures trust must include elements such as integrity, responsibility and open communication, freedom of expression, dialogue, benevolence, dignity, responsibility, accountability, respect of diversity, and mutual understanding.

Secondly, and closely related to the previous one, the leader is responsible for the team's composition, in terms of selecting to "ride the bus" only with members who are trustworthy and eager to trust others, leaving out those who are not. Third, the leader, having the first and last word on setting the organizational rules, norms, and procedures, must secure open communication, acceptance of diverse opinions, and transparency in decision making. Fourth, the leader must encourage those behaviors which contribute to trust building and group cohesion through reward, and discourage those behaviors that can potentially result in catastrophe through punishment. Finally, the leader can create opportunities for social interaction among team members which can contribute to the development of mutual understanding and reinforcement of trust, such as social events, team building workshops, or 360-degree feedback.

As far as the organizational trust is concerned, the leader's responsibility is clearly dependent on the occupied level in the hierarchy, and the magnitude of exposure and transactions with external partners. When the previously analyzed factors that constitute individual trust between leaders and followers, such as integrity, consistency, honesty, ability, benevolence, transparency, open communication, and responsibility, become organizational traits, they add to the development of a trust climate in all the stakeholders of the organization (see Table 7.6). Besides, leaders' high place in the organizational hierarchy is normally associated with an involvement in the designation of organizational structures, processes, policies, and systems. Indeed, if the emphasis of the organizational structures is placed on self-interest, acquisition, and prosperity, neglecting the greater good, and partnership (through shared vision, planning, and resources), then mistrust is more likely to settle. When it comes to managing human resources systems and policies, leaders need to be constantly aware of keeping the promises made and not breaching the psychological contract.

Perhaps the most important element for establishing organizational trust is the encouragement of upward communication processes and mechanisms, as manifest by climate surveys, focus group, conferences, and open-door meetings. All these techniques have been found to promote employees' open and free expressiveness of feelings, perceptions, ideas, problems, expectations, fears, and concerns; thus eliminating the likelihood of a silence climate that impairs trust. Furthermore, organizational trust is also referred to as trust between the organizational units, functions, departments, and teams. The leader, among others, is the liaison between their own team or unit and the rest of the organization and therefore has the responsibility of ensuring the cross-functional trust. The latter emerges in conditions of honest communication, mutual understanding and respect, transparency, procedural fairness. and cross-functional cooperation, thus resulting in a boundaryless organization where effective coordination and integration of organizational units, flexibility, and the organizational learning are prioritized.

Finally, another form of organizational trust can be associated with the organization's policies to actively comply with the spirit of law, ethical standards and international norms. The large numbers of corporate ethical scandals and the abundant instances of business malpractice threaten and violate the trustworthiness of modern organizations. Indeed, the way customers, employees, investors, stakeholders, and all other members of the public view the organization is based on the integrity, accountability, and benevolence of that particular company. Therefore, we can safely argue that the general feeling of trust in an organization is very much dependent upon the perceived corporate social responsibility (CSR).

Table 7.6   How leaders build trust in the organization

- Create an ethical climate and a culture of trust, keep promises concerning the psychological contracts.
- Develop Human Resources management systems which ensure fairness.
- Create upward and cross-functional communication mechanisms with other stakeholders.
- Set rules and procedures that ensure transparency and compliance with ethics.
- Ensure the corporate social responsibility.

There is No Organizational Trust without Socially Responsible Leaders

An organization cannot endure and be profitable unless society prospers, the environment is being preserved, and the economy flourishes. The bottom line is that the organization survives because of the society and the environment. Therefore, it has to become an active and constructive part of the society in which it operates and be responsible for the sustainability of the environment (social and natural). The free capital markets became ruthless in pursuing short-term profits, while the sustained success of the company and the long-term economical prosperity seem to exponentially deteriorate. When combining all the above with the frequently occurring ethical scandals and the global fiscal crisis, it is only natural to observe a reduction of trust in the institution of the organization and an increased pressure for higher CSR.

Social responsibility does not mean that an organization has to give through charities in the context of public relations and social marketing, but instead it denotes an organization that stands as a value creator and not as a value appropriator.[17] CSR means that the management feels responsible and achieves the balancing of multiple stakeholders' needs and perspectives in order to contribute to society's welfare in the short and long term as well as to the sustainability of the environment and the planet.[18] A socially responsible company, then, is responsible to its stakeholders (investors, workers, customers, suppliers, and so on), and ethically accountable for the broad effects of its business activities by aiming to deliver societal and environmental value, sustainability and accountability, and transparency.

The discussion on whether corporate responsibility is merely a trend which absorbs funds from other profitable investments and eventually turns against stakeholders is quite extensive. Furthermore, critics argue that CSR distracts from the economic role of businesses, and pre-empts the role of governments as a watchdog over powerful multinational corporations. However, empirical studies do not seem to account for this stance. On the contrary, they report that investing in CSR either has a neutral financial impact or a positive one. Porras and Collins, drawing evidence from the "Built to

---

17 Ghoshal, S., Bartlett, C., & Peter, M. (1999). A new manifesto for management—Managers need to define their companies as value creators rather than as value appropriators. *Sloan Management Review*, 40(3), 9–20.

18 Kakabadse, N.K., Rozuel, C., & Lee-Davis, L. (2005). Corporate social responsibility and stakeholder approach: A conceptual review. *International Journal of Business Governance and Ethics*, 1(4), 277–302.

Last" companies, suggest that short-term earnings and goals and long-term societal responsibility do not have to be mutually exclusive.[19] In addition, the "Built to Last" companies do not prioritize the maximization of shareholder's profits. Moreover, there is evidence that socially responsible companies are gaining a leverage in attracting skilful, ethical, and talented employees and honest and ethical suppliers, therefore increasing their own competitiveness and value.

As follows, the socially responsible decisions and practices of a company become the essential pillars around which the company builds trust, reputation, and brand name. The employees, as members of the wider social communities, cannot trust the visions and values as declared by their business leaders without making sure that those leaders are socially responsible. In the same vein, the consumers, also occupying the dual role of being members of society, are interested in the protection and the sustainability of the natural and social environment; if they are not convinced that the company is truly socially responsible, they do not maintain their loyalty or preference. The same applies to the other primary and secondary stakeholders. Thus, in order for the leaders to ensure the others' trust in them and in the organization, they must demonstrate in action, their social responsibility. This literally means:

- They go "the extra mile" beyond the passive compliance with the laws and rules of corporate governance and of the charity actions for window-dressing purposes.

- They stand by their decisions in a compass of ethic norms.

- They engage in systematic, transparent and open communication, consultation, and cooperation with the primary and secondary stakeholders.

- They integrate social responsibility into core business and management processes, structures, strategies, and culture.

- They integrate ethical, social, and environmental criteria in decision making, concerning investment, R&D, new products, new services, new technologies, and new markets that meet the multiple stakeholders' societal and environmental needs.

---

19 Collins, J.C., & Porras, J.I. (1994). *Built to Last: Successful habits of visionary companies*. New York: Harper.

- They set goals and measured results concerning the social responsibility actions of the organization and publicly report on them in a consistent and transparent manner.

The Virtuous Circle of Effective Leadership and Trust: Bringing it All Together

The relationship between trust and effective leadership is mutual. Research suggests that through their effective leadership behavior and style, leaders can earn the followers' trust. At the same time, followers perceive the leaders' behavior as effective and are willing to follow him or her as a result of their trust in them. A virtuous circle between effective leadership and the followers' trust that reinforces these two dimensions is created.

Many leadership theories have examined the impact of trust on performance, commitment, and employee well-being, but transformational and ethical leadership theories have placed trust at the core of their conceptualization. So, for example, transformational leaders are perceived as benevolent and consequently more trustworthy as a result of the following four aspects.

First, transformational leaders provide an idealized influence when they demonstrate an exemplary, ethical behavior, including the implicit adoption of personal goals that are not self-centered and have the willingness and ability to pursue these goals, even though doing so may incur personal cost and sacrifice. In addition, they act as role models and demonstrate a kind behavior that is admired by their followers.

By intellectual stimulation, the leaders develop and encourage their followers' independent, innovative, and creative thinking. They encourage followers to ask questions, detect problems, reflect on their goals and jobs, and try to figure out ways of completing their prescribed tasks. This behavioral dimension of leadership increases the perceived integrity, ability, and benevolence of the leaders and enhances the trust of their followers who perceive it as a learning opportunity.

The followers' inspirational motivation can be achieved when their leaders provide them with a sense of purpose and meaning in their job which generates a goal-directed energy. They do that by establishing a vision, awakening commitment to that vision, and setting and communicating precise, clear, and plausible strategies for attaining it. Moreover, they generate realistic optimism among followers who, with the available resources and efforts, are convinced that the goals can be achieved and the vision attained. This behavior relieves the fears, the uncertainty, and the risk of followers to quitting or losing faith, and enhances their trust in the leader and in themselves.

By individualized consideration, the leader demonstrates genuine care for the followers' well-being. They do this by open and adequate interpersonal communication, mentoring, attentive listening to their concerns, needs, fears, and expectations, and by proactively taking decisions to address those issues. This leadership behavior makes followers perceive the leaders as benevolent, something that, in return, generates respect and trust. Reversely, research shows that, as long as followers trust their leader, the more the leadership behavior is effective in the sense that it positively influences behavior and attitude, such as the followers' satisfaction, commitment, organizational, and citizen behavior, and, as a result, high performance.

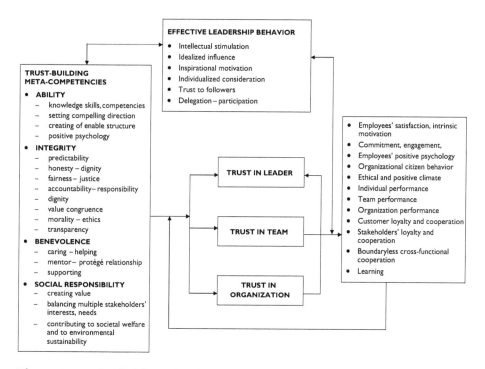

Figure 7.1   Definitions, levels, and outcomes of trust

Concluding Thoughts

Finally, another dimension of this virtuous cycle is that the followers' trust in the leader reinforces the leader's own confidence in the followers and that, in turn, is reflected in the leader's openness, appreciation, and free communication with the followers. This feeling of mutual trust is of particular importance since it makes the followers feel safe, allows them to communicate freely and encourages them to speak up and to report negative feedback, and to participate in the decision-making and the delegation processes.

In a nutshell, the art of building trust should not be something that "just happens" reactively, thoughtlessly, or invisibly. If we don't bring trust to the forefront, the normal chaos of business becomes even more turbulent as we spin erratically and unpredictably in a world of distrust. Figure 7.1 describes the virtuous cycle, the main benefits resulting from trust, and the accompanying factors that define it.

Chapter 8

Developing Leadership Meta-Competencies as Organizational Traits

Introduction—From Individual Traits to Organizational Traits

Individual traits and character, values, motives, and competencies determine the choices, actions, attitudes, and behaviors of leaders through which they determine the being and becoming of the organization. At the same time, the leader is dependent on the organizational context, which encompasses strategies, structures, processes, authority and control mechanisms, systems, culture, and technology which in turn are dependent, to a certain degree, on the organization's external environment. We can therefore assume the organization as an open system, composed of interrelated elements and characteristics, which affect and are affected by the external environment.

As follows, the nature of the organization defines the leadership style, competencies, and behavior. This becomes clear when we pause for a moment to reflect on whether it is possible to have transformational authentic leadership in an organization with bureaucratic structures, processes, controls, and culture, characterized by low levels of initiative, trust, and flexibility. It is then safe to argue that the nature of organization is the cause of the leadership. At the same time, though, we know that the leadership determines the nature of the organization. The choices leaders make affect the strategies, structures, processes, culture, and other organizational aspects and traits. All the above underline the fact that the relationship between organization and leadership is constantly interactive and reciprocal. Taking this thought further, we can assume that leaders' individual traits and meta-competencies can turn into organizational traits. For example, leaders' integrity, phronesis, character, trustworthiness, and mindfulness cannot flourish within an organizational context that doesn't favor or support them. So, leaders not only need to develop those personal traits and competencies for themselves, but also need to convert them into organizational traits.

Indeed, research seems to confirm that leaders, especially those in the upper echelon, bear the main responsibility for the culture of the organization. So, for example, Collins and Porras, studying the "built to last companies," argue that leaders are "clock builders" and not "time tellers," meaning that they take an architectural approach and concentrate on building the organizational traits of visionary companies that can prosper far beyond the pressure of any single leader.[1] Furthermore, according to the research of Kotter and Heskett, the ultimate act of leadership is to institutionalize a leadership-centred culture, where the business rewards people who successfully develop leaders.[2] The same idea is supported by Senge, who asserts that leaders bear the responsibility for modelling a learning organization which is continually expanding its capacity to create its future. All of this means that the basic role of the leader is that of an architect or designer, building an organization where people can continually expand their capabilities in order to understand, learn, improve, and create.[3] These empirical suggestions are in line with the theoretical premise that leaders set the context within which organizational members strive for excellence and work together to achieve organizational and perhaps personal goals.

This responsibility gives the leader three specific roles to fulfil: first, to create a leadership culture within the organization; second, to develop others to become leaders; third, to develop their own self. We shall now present the ideas and proposals that result from the bibliography related to these issues. It is useful though, before proceeding any further, to understand the issues of organizational and leadership culture, given that the latter is the organic sub-total of the former.

The Meaning of Organizational Culture

Corporate culture is a system of common values, beliefs, principles, assumptions, notions, and meanings which compose a common framework of reference that defines people's way of thinking, behaving and communicating, actions, and motivations. All these characteristics (values, principles, beliefs, and so on), are actualized through rules, which strongly determine the individual and team decisions and behavior in a daily basis.[4] These rules function as expectations

---

1   Collins, J., & Porras, J. (1994). *Built To Last: Successful habits of visionary companies*. New York: HarperCollins.
2   Kotter, J., & Heskett, J. (1992). *Corporate Culture and Performance*. New York: The Free Press.
3   Senge, P. (1990). The leader's New York: Building learning organizations. *Sloan Management Review*, Fall, 7–23.
4   Schein, E. (1992). *Organizational Culture and Leadership*. San Francisco, CA: Jossey Bass.

on which attitudes and patterns of behavior are considered appropriate or not within the organization. They are socially preset norms that help us interpret and evaluate behavior and beliefs. The following experiment, conducted at the University of Berkeley, may give an insight into the meaning of culture as rules and the rules as standards of socially expected behavior. The researchers placed cameras in public rest rooms (lavatories) in order to count the number of people washing their hands before exiting. They found out that, when there were two or more persons in the rest room at the same time, 90 percent of them washed their hands. When alone in the lavatories, only 10 percent washed their hands. Why is it that when there is another individual in the rest room we force ourselves to wash our hands, while when alone, we don't? What drives us? It is very unlikely that we would ever find ourselves in a company of a stranger in public lavatories who remarks, "Please sir, wash your hands or I will not allow you to leave the toilets?" The answer is that we know others expect us to wash our hands and, moreover, that if we don't we risk being characterized as dirty. Washing our hands in the rest room thus constitutes a rule or a socially expected behavior which results from the value of cleanliness in our world.

The organizational culture constitutes an intangible strategic resource of the organization since it shapes the individual, team, and overall organizational decisions, attitudes, and behaviors. It can be regarded as a compass that reduces uncertainty and, whilst there is an absence of cause and effect in the literature, there is enough in the current theory to take the view that leaders shape culture and culture shapes leadership behavior through the following:

- identification of appropriate and inappropriate behavior;

- differentiation between significant and insignificant, that is, what is considered a priority, what leaders pay attention to, measure, and control;

- reaction to critical incidents, for example, if an element of the culture is integrity, it means that the leader will maintain an ethical attitude throughout the problem-solving process.

Corporate culture is also expressed in dress code, the layout of the offices, the communication format, and in rituals and ceremonies. Corporate culture functions as a mental framework shared by all members of the organization. For example, the basic elements of the culture of General Electric are speed, simplicity, continuous learning-improvement, the absence of closed doors and strict boundaries between the various organizing teams, few hierarchical levels, and so on. The main elements of the culture at Southwest Airlines are an emphasis on people, a pleasant, casual working environment, low cost flights, and high-quality customer service. 3M fosters a culture of innovation and encourages a continuous quest for new solutions.

Let us look at the characteristics of corporate cultures. Firstly, extent, which reflects the degree to which culture is spread and shared among the members of the organization. If, for instance, an organization claims it has a team culture, to what degree have the values of trust, integrity, and cooperation become understood and embraced by all members? A second basic property of corporate culture is its intensity. Intensity is the degree to which the values, beliefs, principles, and unwritten rules exercise influence and determine the decisions, attitudes, and the members' behavior. A culture is considered strong when people feel they are internally driven and committed to following and applying the values, beliefs, and unwritten informal rules of corporate culture. If, for example, an employee refuses to execute an order given by the managing director because she or he perceives that the order violates the principle of transparency, which is a highly valued aspect of culture, then indeed, the organizational culture can be regarded as very strong. A third property of corporate identity concerns its appropriateness. This characteristic examines the degree to which the culture contributes to the efficient goal attainment and the continuous success of the company.

At this point, it is essential to clarify that the existence of a single corporate culture does not de facto exclude the parallel existence of differentiations in certain elements among the culture of its various organizing units. For example, the dominant element in the finance department may be the emphasis on details and on the accurate presentation of data, while for the sales department it may be customer service, and for the production department, the quality of the product. These differentiations are derived from the nature of the work and operations of every organizational unit. But, overall, these differentiations are compatible with the overall culture.

In addition, in the case of multinational companies, there might be a strong corporate culture, characterized and distinguished by core values, beliefs, notions, and so on which apply internationally. At the same time though, the subsidiary's culture may, if not must, have its own character—on one hand, to incorporate the shared elements of the corporate culture and on the other, to include the "local" elements in such a way as to be adapted to the particularities and the culture of the country in which it is established. Consequently, apart from the corporate culture which affects the whole organization, the notion of sub-culture is equally important since it expresses the differentiated— but compatible with the corporate—cultures, which exist in organizational units, hierarchical levels, geographical regions, and so on, depending on the particularities and the demands of each business and of its environment.

The Organizational Culture as a Source of Competitive Advantage or Disadvantage

The importance of corporate identity stems from its own definition. Culture provides the conceptual framework which demarcates behavior and determines decisions. Practically, it makes clear to organizational members what is significant and insignificant, what is right and wrong, fair and unfair, appropriate and inappropriate, urgent and not so urgent, and so on. At the bottom line, it expresses "the way things are done in a business." In other words, culture determines the decisions, choices, priorities, attitudes, and behaviors of organizational members in respect to issues of strategy, such as innovation and learning.

Depending of the kind of corporate culture adopted, the organization can either gain a considerable competitive advantage or, alternatively, can be a source of competitive disadvantage. For instance, J. Welch of General Electric promoted values such as speed, simplicity, confidence, high goal-setting, boundaryless structures, and continuous improvement, which led to the reduction of bureaucracy and augmented the ability for quick adjustment, immediate responses to changes, flexibility, and continuous learning and improvement. These elements were judged to be of particular importance for the competitiveness and success of a company with 250,000 employees. In the same vein, Herb Kolleher, head of Southwest Airlines, managed to create a strong culture with the basic ingredients of a pleasant and fun atmosphere ("work should be fun ... it can be play ... enjoy it") and the emphasis on people ("People are important ... each one makes a difference").[5] These elements form a working environment and atmosphere in which people achieve high results while experiencing high levels of satisfaction and commitment, despite the fact that their wages are lower than the industry average. This gives Southwest the advantage of being competitive cost-wise, maintaining low prices while at the same time providing high-quality customer and passenger service. As hard as

---

5 Assessing Corporate Culture—Southwest Airlines. (2007). *WriteWork.com*. Retrieved 15 February 2013 from http://www.writework.com/essay/assessing-corporate-culture-southwest-airlines-1.

competitors tried, they failed to imitate the Southwest Airlines culture since culture cannot be copied, at least not easily. In contrast to these examples, there are many businesses with a strong, inappropriate culture—something which can be the source of a series of competitive disadvantages. For instance, IBM's strong culture obstructed the company from making a timely adjustment, and thus its competitors managed to outperform and jeopardize its survival at a time when IBM was the dominant leader in its field.

Indeed, when corporate culture is strong and diffused, meaning completely adopted by all members and appropriate for achieving organizational goals, it can have particularly positive effects on the sustainability and competiveness of the company. Specifically, corporate culture contributes to the effective materialization and formation of a strategy. Indeed, strategy demands an appropriate, matching culture. For example, it is not possible to materialize a competition strategy based on innovation and quality if the company's culture does not favor the quest for new ideas and solutions. When people are afraid of taking initiative and of making mistakes they don't prioritize quality, and innovation is far from being a reference point for decisions and behaviors. For example, since the beginning of the last century, 3M has been a successful and innovative company which is able to grow and compete as a result of its innovative products. The effective materialization of this strategy is based on a corporate culture which encompasses the elements of creativity, entrepreneurship, and a continuous quest for innovations from the entire organization. There are many examples of companies with very clever strategies that failed because they lacked appropriate culture. For example, United, America West, and USair all tried to copy Southwest's strategy, along with its policies and systems. But that they all failed because of a lack of appropriate relative culture. Similarly, the failure of a great number of mergers and acquisitions can be attributed to the inability to manage the coming together of various cultures, despite the fact that the strategic decisions were very well planned and executed. Research shows that two-thirds of mergers and acquisitions do not achieve their goals because intangible (or soft) issues, mainly culture, are not given the required attention. There have been lots of cases of private and public companies hiring expensive, well-known business advisors who devised some very "smart" strategies for them. None of these were effectively materialized though, due to a lack of appropriate corporate culture.

THE CORPORATE CULTURE REINFORCES THE COMMITMENT AND THE MOTIVATION OF THE PEOPLE

If you meet people who are proud of the organization for which they work, and love and fight for its success and you ask them why they feel that way, the chances are that they will not answer that it is because of their salaries. Usually, they respond that is that it's about a "healthy" organization that respects people and is characterized by a pleasant atmosphere, and a feeling of collaboration and trust. The majority of people want to work for an organization of which they can feel proud, that they feel expresses who they are, and gives them a sense of belonging. Culture is one of the essential ingredients forming the image and identity of an organization which gives people a sense of "community." The more the culture of the organization matches the beliefs and values of the individual, the stronger the sense of belonging, identification, commitment, and loyalty will be. Porras and Collins, in their book *Built to Last*,[6] use various examples to demonstrate that extraordinary businesses owe part of their sustained success to the fact they have a strong culture, resembling a "cult or religion" (cult-like culture) which is embraced by their workers. Professor O'Reily, in one of his speeches, gave an extreme but highly didactic example in order to explain the effect of corporate culture on people's commitment and mobilization. It concerned the religious movement called The Unification Church, which has members often called Moonies, a nickname derived from the Church's founder, Sun Myung Moon. In this sect, members offer their time and work without any pay in return. They even offer their incomes. Why do they do that? Apparently because they identify with and deeply believe in the values, principles, convictions, and beliefs of the organization. To avoid any misunderstanding, we do not suggest that, in order for businesses to succeed, they need to follow the examples of churches and sects. O'Reily's example is brought up to strengthen the argument that identification with values, beliefs, principles and, in general, a company's culture, has a positive impact on an individual's commitment to it, as well as on their efforts to achieve the company's targets.

THE CULTURE ENSURES INDIVIDUAL INITIATIVE AND SELF-CONTROL

The organizational culture can provide two important elements for the competitiveness and sustained success of a company in a contemporary environment. First, it promotes disciplined thinking and action without external controls. Supposing that the overall success of the organization requires people's appropriate behaviors, we further assume that there are two ways to ensure the adoption of the right attitudes. First, through external control, which is usually achieved through hierarchy, supervision, and bureaucracy (written rules, procedures, job descriptions, signatures, and so on). For example, maintaining

---

6   Collins, J.C., & Porras, J.I. (1997). *Built to Last: Successful habits of visionary companies.* New York: Harper Business.

a daily timetable can be ensured through a "card" control system or through supervision of employees. A second way is by cultivating self-control, meaning that people realize the importance of following the rules; they have understood what the appropriate behaviors are, the frameworks into which they can move, and through self-discipline they accept and adhere to them out of free will and not of obedience to a higher authority. The second way is preferable for many reasons but, from an organization point of view, this is mainly because it has been found that an authentic, unconstrained, and enthusiastic workforce renders the organization much more efficient. Think, for example, how difficult it would be for an employee to smile warmly and wholeheartedly, produce innovative ideas, or work happily and productively as a member of team, merely out of adherence to the company's rules and policies or for fear of losing their job. Creativity, innovation, passion, and enthusiasm cannot be the outcome of forced methods of bureaucracy, supervision, and hierarchy. These can only be attained if the employee believes in them and is disposed toward attaining them.

A strong culture, on one hand, ensures self-discipline, responsibility, and self-control and, on the other, gives people freedom to use their own judgment and creativity, to take initiative, to work fast and flexibly, with enthusiasm and zest, without rigid bureaucratic and hierarchical rules, and need for approval and restrictions. J. Collins, in his book *Good to Great*, dedicates a chapter to this positive outcome of corporate culture. He supports that "disciplined people need less hierarchy, disciplined thinking needs less bureaucracy and disciplined action needs less controls."[7] Collins also thinks that great businesses are characterized by a discipline culture beyond the fact that it's the same strong culture that contributes to discipline. A similar discipline culture was created by Otto Rehhagel, the coach of the Greek national football (soccer) team which, combined with the players' passion and strength, led to the team winning the European Championship in 2004.

Besides serving as a tool for self-control and discipline, corporate culture is a powerful mechanism of social control. When a team shares jointly accepted values, beliefs, principles, and so on, then each member of the team is being forced, by the rest of the team, to adopt the culture, attitudes, and behaviors. When a team member violates some of the elements of the culture, his or her behavior becomes apparent and is undesirable to most of the other team members who "press" for compliance. Think again of the experiment which looked at hand washing in public rest rooms.

---

7   Collins, J.C. (2001). *Good to Great: Why some companies make the leap—and others don't*. New York: HarperBusiness.

To conclude, strong culture allows the partial replacement of the administrative-exterior control mechanisms (hierarchy, bureaucracy) by social control and self-control. Apart from the aforementioned consequences on employees' free expression, the partial replacement of the external control mechanisms (supervisors), results in a considerable reduction of administrative cost.

CULTURE REDUCES SOCIAL UNCERTAINTY AND LEADS PEOPLE TOWARD A COMMON DIRECTION AND COOPERATION

Corporate culture, among other things, reduces social uncertainties and leads people toward a common direction, contributing significantly to the coordination, synchronization, cohesion, and collaboration between organizational members. The common values, convictions, notions, meanings, principles, and unwritten rules create common standards criteria to all employees in relation to what is right or wrong, good or bad, important or insignificant, urgent or not. Uncertainty is reduced because employees do not have to guess or doubt what are the appropriate or inappropriate decisions and behaviors. This common reference framework allows organizational members to cooperate efficiently and cultivate a feeling of belonging to a community. Let's take a thought experiment for a moment. A has a common culture with B and is different from C. All three set up an appointment to meet in downtown Athens on Tuesday night, without setting either the time or the place. Which ones have more chance of meeting each other? The odds are in favor for A meeting with B as a result of their shared culture, which tends to reduce uncertainty regarding the place and the time of their meeting. So, given the great complexity and insecurity of the modern business world, reducing uncertainty and promoting coordination, cooperation, and mutual adjustment among people, are required more than ever before. Particularly in the case of international and multinational companies, the shared corporate culture matched with the sub-cultures of the company's units and of the national cultures, is a crucial factor for establishing a common future.

CULTURE CAN FACILITATE OR OBSTRUCT CHANGE AND ADAPTABILITY

The existence of a powerful culture can lead to dogmatism, rigidness, and consequently to negative attitudes concerning the necessary changes for the adjustment and the progress of the company. One such example is IBM's strong culture (IBM's way), as well as the culture of public organizations with rigid bureaucratic structures. It's been documented through several research studies that a strong culture is the most difficult organizational aspect to change.

Moreover, it has been found that more often than not the main cause for the failure of change implementation plans comes down to the fact that those changes were not attempted in parallel with a culture change. On the opposite side, there are businesses where corporate culture facilitates constant change and adaption, because it contains elements such as innovativeness, entrepreneurship, continuous learning and improvement, risk taking, proactiveness, vigilance, and so on. Continuous success requires a culture that will not allow complacency or resistance to change but will also make people want to pursue continuous progress and innovation, believing that "good is never enough."

The Leadership Culture

Having introduced the general aspects of organizational culture, which are further related to leadership culture, we can now proceed with defining leadership culture as an organizational trait. So, leadership culture is a system of shared values, beliefs, principles, assumptions, and meanings that characterize leaders and leadership process within the organization. Specifically, leadership culture is concerned with the following interrelated issues.

Firstly, leadership culture is determined by the way the organization favors and desires the *raison d'être* of leaders and leadership. Practically, at this point leadership culture addresses the core elements and distinguishing factors of the existence of the organization:

- What needs should leaders and leadership satisfy, and how?

- Which future direction is prioritized—short-term, or long-term results, or both?

- Is leadership a core competence and critical factor for the sustained success of the organization?

- Are leaders and leadership concerning only with the upper levels or all organizational levels?

The second issue regards which leadership styles and behaviors the organization favors and desires. The questions here concern the "how" of leadership. In order to reply to this question, academic literature can be a very good starting point. So, some elements can be drawn from the various proposed theories such as transformational, authentic, ethical, and servant leadership, which have widely been analyzed in bibliography. It must be noted here that, apart from leaders' history and personality that determine the style adopted, management schools have a major role to play. Since a great part of today's leading figures have graduated from business schools, the latter can be regarded accountable, at least to a certain degree, for the leadership styles they promote.

The third issue that shapes leadership culture is related to the question about the being of the leader, meaning the leader's character, personality dimensions, traits, skills, and competencies. The link to the previous issue is apparent. For example, if leadership culture is formulated around the premises of ethical leadership, it's not possible that the integrity and morality of the leaders are not part of it. If the *raison d'être* of the leader is the creation of value for the balanced satisfaction of all for the stakeholders' interests, it is not possible that phronesis is not part of the leadership culture. If the desired element of leadership culture is authentic leadership, then elements such as existential intelligence, self-awareness, or mindfulness cannot but be parts of it.

The fourth issue concerns how the organization creates the conditions for leaders to exercise leadership and develop themselves.

Each organization ought to have a visible leadership culture, aligned with its purpose, mission, strategies, businesses activities, technologies, and the characteristics of its environment. Ulrich notes that the leadership models adopted by companies often fall short because they are not linked to customers, shareholders, and business results. He proposes the term "leadership brand" in order to provide the theoretical connection between leaders' attributes and the results. Specifically, "leadership brand is a reputation for developing exceptional managers with a distinct set of talents that are uniquely geared to fulfil customers' and investors' expectations. A company with a leadership brand inspires faith that employees and managers will consistently make good on the firm's promises."[8]

All the above confirm that the transformation of the desired and suitable leadership is the leaders' responsibility, especially of those belonging to the upper echelon. They are the ones who have to choose and set the basic elements for every one of the already mentioned axes, in a way as to ensure that the continuous effective leadership remains one core organizational competence, which shall be the source for competitive advantage and will secure the sustained success of the organization. Equally important to the definition of a

---

8   Urlich, D., & Smallwood, N. (2003). *Why the Bottom Line Isn't*. New York: John Wiley and Sons.

suitable leadership culture, is the leaders' role on its establishment in order for it to become a core component of the organizational DNA.

Shaping the Leadership Culture

The leadership culture, like the organizational culture, is formulated in two ways: first, through its members' interactions during the lifetime and evolution of the organization, and, second, through its designed implementation or change. The first way is somehow non-conscious, or even random. It can be based, for example, on critical events that take legendary dimensions, on the repetition of decisions and behaviors that are converted into doctrines and rules. Furthermore, the organization's founder expresses and influences the organizational culture as a result of their mentality, convictions, values, beliefs, assumptions, and principles. These, in turn, are spread out to the partners, but they are not generally accepted or established until there is sufficient evidence that they support the efficiency and success of the business idea and objectives.[9] For example, the founders of Walt Disney and Hewlett Packard left their mark on the cultures of the businesses they founded for decades. Further, culture is shaped by the experiences and learning process of the organization. Notions, attitudes, and behaviors, though their repetitive usage may be established, especially the successful ones that function as credos, convictions, values, and unwritten rules. Furthermore, people working in teams shape the nature and operation of an organization through their interactions, common experiences, common values, notions, interpretations, standards, convictions, assumptions, and so on. The way a corporate culture is established through interaction and experiences during the organizational evolution can be highlighted by the following experiment:

Four monkeys were introduced into the same cage and a banana was placed in the middle of it. The monkeys, having a thing for bananas, rushed to grab it. At that moment, a guard began to shower them with lots of water which hit them with high pressure with the purpose of preventing them from taking the banana. The monkeys stopped trying to get banana, forced back by the pain of being hit by high-pressure water. As soon as the guard stopped hitting them with water, the monkeys recovered and started reclaiming the banana. The guard went through the same process over and over again until the monkeys learned that "we don't touch the banana." As a result, no matter

---

9   Child, J. (1997). Strategic choices in the analysis of actions, structures organizations and environment: Restrospect and prospect. *Organizational Studies*, 18(1), 43–76.

how many bananas were placed in their cage, the monkeys did not attempt to get to them. Some time later, they removed one of the monkeys from the cage and replaced it with a new one; this new one, as soon as she saw the banana, rushed to get it since there was no way of knowing what had previously happened. But, now a new behavior was observed; the other three monkeys started beating the new one because they didn't want that pressurized water to hit them again. From this, even the new monkey learned that she should not touch the banana. Then the second of the old monkeys was removed and replaced with another one who also rushed to get the banana and got beaten by the others; again, the second monkey learned not to touch the banana. Then the third of the old monkeys was replaced with another one who also rushed to grab the banana and ended up beaten by the others, so the third one also learned, "we don't touch the banana;" the fourth monkey out of the original four was finally replaced and the new one also learned her lesson: "we don't touch the banana." The interesting outcome of this experiment is that, of the monkeys remaining in the cage, none had been sprayed with pressurized water and, therefore, they do not know why they have to beat up the monkey who dares to reclaim the banana! But, inside the cage, the rule is "we don't touch the banana," without any of the monkeys knowing the reason.

The moral of the above story is that it highlights the fact that, through interaction, experience, repetition, and the course of evolution, an organization establishes its culture. We have indeed encountered many businesses where there are rules such as, "in here, we don't touch the banana" and when asking, "why?" the answer is, "because that's the way we do things here." These behaviors have been created at some point of time, have been maintained through repetition and are still valid, regardless of the fact that they might have a negative influence in today's modern environment. This way of shaping culture doesn't ensure the adoption of the appropriate one. In the monkey experiment, it was unreasonable that the last three monkeys would beat up the fourth one without knowing why, since they never experienced being sprayed by the water. It becomes apparent, then, that leadership culture is too serious a strategy to be left to chance.

The Leader as Leadership Culture Creator

The leaders' role in designing and implementing leadership culture can be specified first at the level of actions that are planned and are taking place at the organization level and second at the leaders' individual level. At the first level, the actions that need to be planned and implemented are the following:

1. *Diffusion of culture.* The first action in designing and changing leadership culture is to diffuse the elements of the desired culture to the organizational members. The diffusion firstly aims to make organizational members deeply understand the content of the basic elements of the desired culture, such as values, beliefs, principles, and meanings. Secondly, it should make people realize the usefulness and the benefits of these elements for the organization and for themselves. It is very important to make every element of the desired culture as clear as possible. This isn't limited to defining the meaning of each element, but also includes practical application through a thorough description of the specific behaviors that result from the specific elements of the desired culture. For example, if "integrity" is the desired element of the leadership culture, we need to make people understand the content of this value by expressing it in specific and concrete ways. This means, we need to describe what a leader has to do and how he has to behave in order to comply with the value of integrity. It could be that, for example, the value "integrity" practically means reliability, honesty, and transparency— "I mean what I say and I say what I mean"—honesty, fair treatment, keeping to one's principles and values despite difficulties.

    Furthermore, the diffusion of the desired leadership culture demands proper communication by the executives of the organization, especially those at the top. Communicating the desired culture must be mainly realized through clear and concise verbal and interpersonal messages, not only for understanding purposes but also for learning. Communicating the leadership culture becomes more effective when the following are being used:[10]

    - Practical examples that illustrate the leaders' and the leadership behavior elements, mainly the benefits that result from them for the business and the leader.

    - Stories of the past based on facts but adequately processed in order "to pass" the desired culture, philosophy, values, and so on.

    - Myths and legends: Stories told about real or fictitious events of the past, mainly about the founders or the leader–heroes of the

---

10 Schein, E. (1992). *Organizational Culture and Leadership.* San Francisco, CA: Jossey Bass.

company, which demonstrate the "leadership grandeur" and accentuate, in a dramatic way, some of the elements of its culture..

- The corporate dialect (jargon), meaning, terminology, and code, with characteristic words used to express meanings, beliefs, values, and principles (for example, well-known CEO used the word "mudjahedin").

- Symbols such as images, signs, flags, and slogans (for example, "Simply Better" from Smith Kline Beecham) that express the organization's most important values on leadership. For example, Colin Marshal of British Airways appeared unexpectedly one day at the Board of Directors meeting room, wearing a pin that said: "People are my priority." At first the executives laughed, a few months later though, all of them were wearing the same pins.

- Ceremonial procedures, meaning ceremonies, events and festivities, that accentuate that accentuate the elements of the culture of a people and that are passed on from generation to generation. For example, there are businesses that organize ceremonies where rewards are given to members and festivities are held to celebrate important company occasions and successes.

- In addition to all of the above, another important way of spreading or communicating leadership culture is the educational programs which we shall discuss in the following pages.

  - *Supporting culture.* Communicating and understanding leadership culture are necessary and crucial conditions. But they do not guarantee culture formulation or establishment. Culture needs to be accompanied and supported, directly or indirectly, by the human resources policies, functions, and systems, of which the most important are:[11]
  - *Hiring and promotions.* People start working at an age when they already have established their character, mentality, personality, and skills that are transferred into the workplace. So, selection and promotion of those people that match the organization's

---

11 Chatman, J., & Cha, S. (2003). Leading by leveraging culture. *California Management Review*, 45(4), 20–32.

desired leadership culture is a basic mechanism supporting organizational culture. If, for example, the desired element of the organization's culture is maintenance of ethical standards then, apart from the standard qualifications, the basic criteria for hiring new employees would be character, morality, and integrity.

– *Appraisal.* The leader's formal appraisal evaluation of an employee covers, apart from effectiveness, their skills and behaviors. The outstanding performance of an employee is and must be the combination of their performance in both of these sectors. For example, J. Welch of General Electric evaluated leaders on these two sectors, based on the grid shown in Figure 8.1. The ones who exhibited high results and who at the same time were showing exemplary exercise of the values and principles of the company, were rewarded as much as possible with promotions, financial, and non-financial rewards. Employees who scored low and did not apply the company values were removed. The employees who had poor results but who were exemplary in applying the company's values were given a second or even a third chance through counseling and development, assignment to a position more suitable to their profile, and so on. His dilemma concerned those who had particularly high performances in their results but who were very low in the application of the company's values. This was an issue that troubled him a lot, but he ended up deciding that these executives had to be removed from the company because they would not make the organization grow in the way he wished and, therefore, they would not ensure a sustained, continuous course for the future. It seems that Welch was right. Achieving short-term goals is clearly demanding, but if an employee does not support and apply the organizational values, and does not develop and support the culture, they do not contribute to the organization's future or long-term success. For extraordinary businesses achieving sustained success, it is not only the outcome that matters but also the way it has been established. Therefore, in the official appraisal system there must be criteria, skills, and behavior assessments which cover the basic elements of the desired leadership culture.

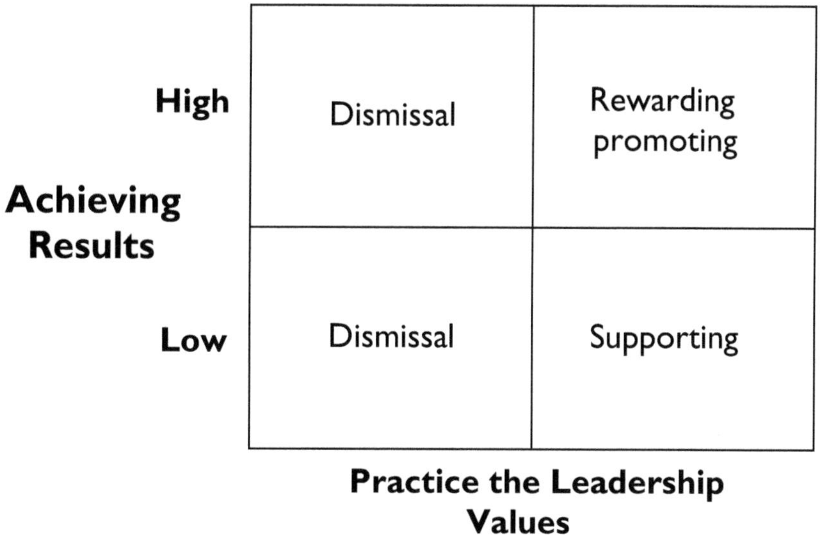

High	Dismissal	Rewarding promoting
Low	Dismissal	Supporting

Achieving Results

Practice the Leadership Values

Figure 8.1   Criteria for leaders' evaluation in General Electric

- *Recognition–rewards*. What is being rewarded and what is being punished in a company expresses what is perceived as important and correct and what is insignificant and wrong. It expresses which behaviors the company values as appropriate and desirable and which are inappropriate and undesirable. Thus, the establishment of the desired leadership culture must be supported by reward and recognition (formal or informal) of the behaviors that are aligned with the desired culture and also by the punishment (ranging from a simple warning to dismissal) of the ones opposing or who are incompatible with the desired culture. The recognition and reward of exceptional leadership behaviors can be achieved through daily positive feedback and praise on behalf of the supervisors, as well as with official remuneration such as annual salary raises, promotions, awards, official praise, and other symbolic rewards.
- *Monitoring*. Establishing the desired leadership culture requires constant monitoring in order to identify the deviations between the adopted and the applied culture and to proceed with the necessary corrective moves. Such practices are the annual performance review of leaders at all levels, 360-degree feedback (through which the opinions and perceptions of followers are expressed), and the undertaking of satisfaction and climate

surveys. These can provide sufficient information on the leaders' results and the effects they have on satisfaction, motivation, inspiration, commitment, trust, and behavior of followers.

- *Practicing the leadership culture.* In addition to diffusing and establishing the desired leadership culture, a leader sets an example by incorporating into his or her own daily routine, both personal and professional. Through repetition, the leadership culture becomes embedded into the mindsets and habits of the leader. Leaders are also role models and ought to teach the organization's desired culture to those followers who are already leaders or will become leaders in the future. At the same time, they ought to ensure (demand and control) that their followers behave according to the leadership culture. This logic is schematically illustrated in Figure 8.2.

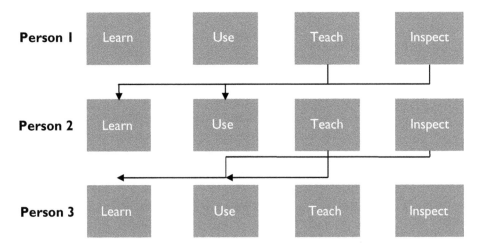

Figure 8.2   How to transfer culture

Leaders Develop Leaders

As already mentioned, the leaders' legacy are the people that stay behind when they leave the organization, the next generation that will make the company succeed and grow. A few years after ending their career, leaders will hardly remember the decisions made or the results achieved but they are likely to remember the people they left behind to carry on with their work. Therefore, the ultimate responsibility of leaders is to create a great leadership culture and to develop great leaders.[12] Apart from becoming role models for the organization, research suggests that leaders undertake a series of developmental activities in order to create a leadership culture and encourage followers' meta-competencies. For these activities to succeed there are two prerequisites that need to be met. First, to identify those followers who might display leadership potential by adequate evaluation of certain traits, such as character, personal traits, motives, competencies, and meta-competencies. Second, based on the specific organization's leadership culture, one can determine the ideal profile of the leader and of the effective leadership behavior. Having clarified those, the developmental activities can focus on the desired individual traits and competencies.

As far as the specific steps that need to be followed, McCall and colleagues have concluded that the key to a leader's development is experience.[13] Through the specific experiential activities listed below, leaders can learn specific skills and develop their "leader's characteristics." So qualities such as self-confidence, persistence, strategic thinking, interpersonal skills, independence, and motivation to exercise leadership can be in followers by their leaders. Specifically, the authors recommend the following activities to develop a leader's growth:

- challenging duties and assignments from the early stages of their career;

- observing very good and very bad leadership role models early on in their career;

- duties and assignments that expand knowledge and experience;

- assignment of special task force duties;

- coaching and mentoring from higher executives;

- attending meetings beyond the scope of their own role;

- special developmental positions (for example, assistant to higher ranked executives);

---

12 Tichy, N., & Cohen, E. (1997). *The Leadership Engine: How winning companies build leaders at every level*. New York: Harper Business.
13 McCall, M.W., Lombardo, M.M., & Morrison, A. (1988). *The Lessons of Experience*. Lexington, MA: Lexington.

- special projects;

- formally designed educational programs.

Research conducted at the Centre for Creative Leadership in the USA showed that, in order to assess their leadership competence, the duties and projects undertaken by potential leaders must be accompanied and characterized by the following challenges:

- successes and failures must be communicated to all and all people have an equal chance to create success and failure;

- the circumstances must include a scenario in which the leader is left alone to confront a problem and has no access to further higher hierarchical levels;

- incorporate collaboration with young people, including either an unusually large number of people or "difficult" people;

- work should be undertaken under particularly stressful conditions;

- the need to influence people over which the leader would not normally have any legal authority;

- confrontation of change, doubt, and uncertainty;

- exercising leadership as head of a team under hectic conditions;

- managing a duty-project which has considerable strategic implementations or is mentally exhausting;

- collaboration with a particularly efficient or particularly inefficient supervisor;

- confronting a situation in which some important factors are missing such as, for example, limited resources;

- hardships such as overloading, making decisions on dismissals, handling bad supervisors and subordinates, failures, mistakes, and handling competitive behaviors.

Discovering and Developing the Hidden Values of the Virtues is a Leader's Responsibility

Albert Camus maintained that life is the sum of our choices, epitomizing the central claim of existential philosophy that existence precedes essence. This means that human beings create their own values and determine meaning in their life and therefore are responsible for what they become. But, human beings—and this is the main criticism concerning existentialism—do not live in an isolated and controlled environment. British sociologist Anthony Giddens argued for the "duality of structure," meaning that the relationship between individuals and social institutions is reciprocal; we create society and we are also the creation of society. Social actors are reflexive and monitor the flow of activities; they adapt their actions to their evolving understandings. They exercise considerable freedom to make their own choices in relation to who they want to become, where to go, how to get there, and how to leave life.

Consequently, and in accordance with the relevant literature, leaders are not born but are mainly becoming, through their life choices. It has been widely supported in the literature, that leadership development is in fact self-development. It can be argued that the notion of self-leadership is the modern version of the Socratic "know thyself," in terms of having a developed sense of who you are, what you can do, and where you are going. Otherwise, it is defined as "the process by which you influence yourself to achieve your objectives".[14] Leadership development is a learning journey and to quote Marcel Proust: "We don't receive wisdom. We must discover it for ourselves after a journey that no one takes for us or spares us."

The Lifelong Learning Journey

In a fast-changing world and environment, the issue of continuing learning and education becomes critical not only for career advancement or enrichment of leadership competences repertoire, but first and foremost for personal development and wellness purposes. But, to begin with, it is important to clarify the meaning of learning. Learning is not about simple knowledge acquisition. Knowledge on its own can be of no use. Smokers, for example, are usually very well-informed about the catastrophic consequences of smoking,

---

14 Kazan, A., & Bryant, A. (2012). *Self-leadership: How to become a more successful, efficient and effective leader from inside out.* New York: McGraw-Hill.

yet they continue to smoke. Returning to the organizational environment, this problematic is of particular value; indeed, we cannot emphasize enough the criticality of constantly being informed. In the absence of learning, organizations and people within it are inclined to repeat old practices, not catching up with technological changes and products. The academic community, acknowledging the link between learning and continuous improvement, have urged for "learning organizations" and "knowledge-creating companies."

Peter Senge, who introduced the term "learning organizations" in his magnificent book *The Fifth Discipline* analyzes learning through the Greek term "metanoia."[15] The verb "μετανοώ" in Greek it means, "I revise my way of thinking and of what I'm doing" or, to put it another way, "I am aware of what I'm doing, why I'm doing it, how I'm doing it and I decide to change it." It literally means a shift in mindset. In the words of Senge, "to grasp the meaning of metanoia is to grasp the deeper meaning of learning, for learning also involves a fundamental shift or movement of the mind." The essence of learning, then, is not taking in information, but instead acquiring the means to learn. Besides, especially in our times where the access to information and potential learning opportunities is endless, learning is about perceiving connections between fields, ideas and concepts. In a broader sense, and in accordance with the premises of the connectivism theory of learning, decision making is itself a learning process. Choosing what to learn and the meaning of incoming information is seen through the lens of a shifting reality. While there is a right answer now, it may be wrong tomorrow as a result of alterations in the information climate affecting the decision.

Therefore, a leaders' development is the constant improving of the meta-competencies as discussed in this book and of the resulting personality traits and competencies. Before we introduce some ideas concerning the leader's learning journey, it might be fruitful to pinpoint a few obstacles that frequently hinder it. The first barrier is related to leaders' egotism or arrogance and the impression that they know all they need to know. This is the opposite of what Socrates supported, that, wise is the man who is aware of the things he knows but also of the things he does not. A second barrier to learning is habit. Naturally we find pleasure in familiar situations, in a specific way of thinking or behaving, and we don't wish to "sail for new waters." To clarify our point, just think: "Which shoes are more comfortable, the new or the old ones?" Most of us will go for the old ones, because we know their shape and

---

15 Senge, P.M. (1990). *The Fifth Discipline. The art and practice of the learning organization.* London: Random House.

sensation and we keep away from the new, which at first might be associated with fear, uncertainty, and agitation. The third obstacle to learning is of extreme importance because it is not easily detectable, in the sense that it is happening to us without us noticing it; it is inertia or inactivity. Usually, the changes in our lives are not dramatic or drastic, but small and invisible, and either we don't realize them or we ignore them because of the numerous stimuli and daily distractions. For example, while you are reading these lines or while you are sleeping, changes are happening in the world. Inertia, then, makes us remain the same—not learning and not adjusting to new circumstances or situations. But, unfortunately, these small changes accumulate one on top of the other, just like rocks which eventually become a wall. Based on this metaphor, we could schematically derive three types of responses. In the first category there are those who don't realize the existence of a wall and run against it and hit hard. In other words, when they realize they have to change, it's already too late. In the second category we find those people who realize there is a wall at the very last moment, and manage to avoid it and survive but with lots of trauma and blows. In the third category of responses there are those people who, while they are on a walk say: "What a nice place this is, let's build a wall for others to crash into." That is why change and learning need to be pursued voluntarily and not reactively or compulsorily by those who lead.

Having briefly presented the obstacles blocking learning, let's move on to the conditions that facilitate learning and the ways leaders can develop themselves and improve traits or competencies in accordance with their personality or character. The fundamental precondition for learning and for personal development is strong willpower or volition, since mere desire is not enough. Returning to the smoking example, almost all smokers want to quit smoking. But only the ones with strong willpower finally make it. Willpower means focusing on what one wants to achieve or learn, setting a goal, and formulating an action plan. It requires commitment, focus, and discipline to realize. Jack Welch was for several decades one of the most important business leaders in North America. He graduated from the best universities and, in order to climb the ladder from being a simple employee to the top of General Electric, an organization with about 250,000 employees, he spent a lot of time in training and learning seminars on administration and leadership. But, in one of his speeches to high corporate executives of the private sector in Greece, he said: "The most important principle of my life, I didn't learn it in MIT or Harvard but it came from my mother. This principle that has marked me both as a human being and as a professional is the following: You simply need to really want it."

For such strong willpower or, as Peter Senge calls it, creative tension for learning to emerge, we need to realize the gap between the "where we stand today"—how we think, which knowledge and skills we have, how we behave and react to situations, what are strengths or weaknesses are—to the "where we want to be." In other words, we need to obtain an accurate perception of our present self and also of our ideal self—who we want to be, what is our personal vision, or our ideal values as leaders. If we are not aware of this gap then the desire for learning and change will not be awoken in us, therefore there will be no need to learn or change anything. If this statement is valid, then a precondition or motivation for learning is self-awareness; hence, we need to become observers of ourselves, and specifically become aware of our emotions, strengths, and weaknesses, as well as our way of thinking, behaving, judging, and socializing. Self-awareness then presupposes introspection and careful reflection. But, our perception of ourselves can be quite different from how other people see us; we usually see ourselves from the place of intention, while others see us from the place of actions. So, in the process of achieving self-awareness, seeking or soliciting feedback takes on a whole new perspective. Distancing ourselves from the emotions (positive or negative) that might accompany feedback or criticism, we can increase our self-awareness just by paying attention to how other people see us. This is consistent with the view of existential philosophers who argue that the individual who engages in existential thinking incorporates in their point of view the "other's point of view."

So, if willpower and a constant drive for self-awareness are there, we can proceed with examining a few ideas on how we learn or on how we can live our life journey through learning. The learning process begins with the clear and precise comprehension of a new knowledge, concept, principle, or theory. In other words, understanding means to have a clear picture of the how and what we can change, improve, or learn. Although understanding of terms, notions, and meanings is a necessary condition for learning, it is not enough for learning to happen. The second stage is acceptance, that is, to accept that it is useful to apply the knowledge notions and theories acquired. The third stage of learning is personal commitment for using and applying the newly acquired knowledge. Finally, the fourth stage is the application of the newly acquired knowledge or practice of a new skill, a new behavior, and so on. At this stage, knowledge transforms to learning for it becomes an undetachable, innate part of ourselves. Take driving for example: at first, we did not know what it required; when we began we realized that it involved a lot more than what we thought, but, if we get committed and believe that it is a useful skill for us to gain, we will be patient and persistent; furthermore, if we don't practice we will never learn to drive; but if we do it over and over again, then the driving ability becomes a part of us and we do it so automatically that we do not have to actively recall the knowledge we acquired during the learning process.

Another approach to learning can be traced back to old times. Confucius, for example, with his well-known phrase, "I hear and I forget, I see and I remember, I do and I understand," set the foundation of experiential learning, which is simply defined as the process of learning from experience. Similarly, Sophocles from 400 BC, noticed that "one must learn by doing the thing, for though you think you know it—you have no certainty, until you try." Aristotle supported that virtue is acquired through repetition. Several great theorists, Dewey and Kolb among them,[16] evolved this linage of thinking and proposed that learning is a process whereby concepts are derived from and continuously modified by experience. In the management and leadership area, there have been many calls to use the assumptions of the aforementioned learning approach, especially in leadership development programs. For example, Day[17] says that "leadership development in practice today means helping people learn from their work rather than taking them away from their work to learn." In addition, continuous and meaningful development of leaders can become reality through "trial and error" and reflection on mistakes, failures, and successes. This requires study, reflection, and questioning in regards to which were the reasons that led to failure or success.

However, even beyond specific instances, like failures and successes, our whole life can be regarded as an ongoing learning experience. By reflecting or reliving in our mind the "scenes we played on stage," we gain a better understanding of situations, and a greater sense of purpose and direction for our lives. Reflection does not solve any current problems but it may help leaders identify better ways to manage the next time. For example, after a lecture, we tend to rewind it in our mind and, at night, before falling asleep, we try to identify those things that could have been presented in a better way, even if there is no indication that the audience did not understand the ideas taught.

A central question though, concerning learning and leadership, regards whether some of a leader's characteristics, such as self-confidence, courage, sensitivity, or dare, can be developed and/or learned. Research findings

---

16 Dewey, J. (1915). Education vs. trade-training. In *John Dewey: The Middle Works* (1979). Carbondale, IL: Southern Illinois University Press, p. 411–413; Kolb, D.A. (1984). *Experiential Learning: Experience as a source of learning and development*. New Jersey: Prentice Hall.

17 Day, D.V. (2000). Leadership development: A review in context. *Leadership Quarterly*, 11(4), 581–613.

conform to our view that the response is positive, as long as willpower and practice are present. Besides, let's not forget Aristotle's idea on virtues, bravery, phronesis, and the quest for perfection. In the philosopher's words, "excellence of character results from habituation (ethos)—which in fact is the source of the name it has acquired (êthikê), the word for 'character-trait' being a slight variation of that for habituation (êthos). This makes it quite clear that none of the excellences of character (êthikê arête) come about in us by nature; for no natural way of being is changed through habituation (ethizetai)."

Concluding Thoughts

In conclusion, someone becomes a leader mainly through the learning journey of his or her life. Human sciences and especially philosophy, psychology, sociology, management, human resources management, and education sciences, offer us lots of knowledge, notions, principles, theories, methods, and techniques to develop leaders. The environment we live in and, in particular, the working environment, also offers us a multitude of opportunities and experiences that we can value.

Index

alienation 23, 26, 45
aloneness 108, 111
amoral 26, 45, 46
apathy 45, 63, 77
Aristotle 52–5, 76–81
artists 25, 48, 68
authenticity 7–9, 30, 65–6
awareness 24, 38
   ethical 48–9
   moral 124–5
   self-awareness 31–2, 63–4, 113–15
   spiritual 27

beliefs 24–35, 120–21, 154–67
Bennis, Warren 83, 105
business schools 22, 82–6

charisma 4, 34
commitment 35, 79–89, 113–23, 135, 158–9
common good 53–7, 60–64
competence 14–20, 26, 32, 143, 162–73
competing interests 12, 47
competitive advantage 131, 157, 163
complexity 124–5
   behavioral 17, 100
   cognitive 118
   ethical 49
   leadership 130
   organizational 66
Confucius 98, 177
consumption 46, 47
contemplation 25–8, 127
corruption 46, 101

cosmos 24–9
courage 72–9, 113–18
creativity 111–12, 118–20
culture 13–22, 34, 37, 63–8, 97, 135–62
   corporate 61, 154–64
   ethical 7, 99
   leadership 154, 162–72
   organizational 154–62

death 24–8
deprivation 29, 46
dilemmas 115
Durkheim 27
duty 23, 55

education 49, 80–85
empower 8, 9, 134
ethical 22–30, 35, 47–63
   behavior 91, 94, 150
   codes 22, 49–51, 86, 101
   culture 81, 99
   decision-making 83
   leadership 5–7, 30, 102, 122–5, 150, 163
   scandal 22, 148
   values 65–6, 141
ethics 5–6, 18, 22, 48–68, 94, 102, 124–5
ethos 58, 178
existential 24, 27, 110
   ability 27
   angst 28
   challenges 46
   concerns 48

contemplation 28
crisis 24–7, 67
despair 27
frustration 43
intelligence 27–32, 163
philosophers 28, 176
philosophy 173
problems 27
quest 26, 43
questions 26, 28, 29, 42
thinking 27–9, 35–44, 68, 176
existentialism 24, 173

followership 71, 90, 134
Frankl, Victor 43
free market dogma 45
freedom 109–21, 173

Gardner, H. 27, 112
George, Bill 7, 41
George, William 98, 114
Ghosal, S. 116, 117
global marketplace 47
global network economy 45
Goleman, D. 114

harmony 17–18, 75, 97
Heidegger 31–2, 110
    Dasein 31
holistic 9, 18, 46, 73, 82, 96
hope 4, 8–10, 41, 144–5
humility 10, 64–5, 77–9
humor 77

ideal 9, 33–5, 54–5, 171
    city 29
    leader 62,
    leadership 3, 66
    regime 29
    self 117, 123, 176
idealized influence 4, 150

identity 8, 31, 114, 123, 159
    corporate 156–7
    self- 73, 109, 118
immoral 22, 45, 94, 96
inconsistency 28, 46, 49, 95–100
individualized 46, 145
    consideration 4–5, 151
inner theatre 105–6
innovation 4, 5, 48, 118–19, 156–62
inspirational 60
    motivation 4, 150–51
integral 67, 93, 95, 100–102, 134, 140
integrity 6, 79, 80, 89–103, 140–42,
    150–68
    behavioral 91, 97, 98
    emotional 91
    moral 50
intellectual stimulation 4, 5, 15, 150

job satisfaction 8, 99, 101
justice 6, 62, 76–9, 140–45

Kierkegaard 26, 110
knowledge era 45
Kubric, Stanley 24

leadership
    authentic 7–9, 30–33, 153, 163
    charismatic 4, 99, 102, 112
    development 33, 41, 86, 173, 177
    effective 2–4, 14, 21, 112–13,
        150–51
    emergence 1, 2, 20
    ethical 5–7, 30, 102, 122–5, 150, 163
    self- 16, 105, 107, 113, 120, 173
    servant 10, 33, 66
    transformational 4–5, 10, 14–15,
        33, 99, 102, 150, 153
learning organization 9, 154, 174
legal 49, 50, 172
loneliness 106–9, 129–30

meaning 32–5
meaningful 9, 22, 26, 32–4, 46–7, 86
mindfulness 36–41, 119
    Langer 38
mischief 49
mismanagement 49
modern management 7, 46
moral debt 46
morality 5, 22–30, 50, 65–8, 94–8, 141
motivation 32–6, 43, 144, 150–51, 170–71
motivational 60, 73–5, 144

Nietzsche 27, 48
Nonaka, I. 51–69

ontology 48
optimism 143–5, 151
organizational environment 57, 174

paradigm shift 22
performance indicators 45
philosophical turn 24–7
philosophy 22–5, 29–30, 46–7, 52–5
phronesis 45–71, 76, 163, 178
Plato 29, 80
political 46–7, 54–67
    circumstances 45
    happenings 45
    leaders 46, 72, 83, 96
    scandals 22, 132
poverty 46, 47, 67
practical wisdom 50–52, 66, 76
problem solving 47, 137
prudence 50, 54, 77
public policy 48
purpose 23–34, 114, 116, 150
    in life 28, 35, 43

raison d'être 11–13, 47, 61, 162–3
reflection 28, 68–9, 82–5, 108–26, 176–7
    self- 31, 43–4, 114

resilience 39–44, 61, 122
resonant leadership 39

sacrifice 4, 10, 54, 66, 150
Seidman, Dov 46
self-confidence 113–24
self-efficacy 40
self-regulation 77, 109, 113, 123, 143
Senge, Peter 117, 120, 154, 174, 176
social norms 111
social responsibility 79, 147–50
solitude 105–30
Solomon, Robert 97
spiritual 23–6, 46, 54, 67
    awareness 27
    leadership 9–10, 30
spirituality 10, 67–8, 110–12
stakeholders 12, 78, 124, 146–51
status quo 5, 118, 143
strategy 157–8
sustainability 6, 52, 142–51
systemic approach 11

traits 1–3, 17–20, 74–6, 113–18,
    130–46, 153–4, 171–5
transcendence 77–80
trust 79–99, 101–2, 131–56
    development 90, 140
    in the leader 134–52

values 31–42, 50–52, 58–76, 90–118,
    141–2, 153–69
    core 30, 31, 66, 98
    creating 47
virtues 19, 50–55, 71–81, 173
    meta-virtue 64, 91
virtuous cycle 46, 152
vision 9–10, 32, 60–64, 112–20, 134,
    143, 150–51

well-being 32–9
Welch, Jack 90

For Product Safety Concerns and Information please contact our EU
representative GPSR@taylorandfrancis.com
Taylor & Francis Verlag GmbH, Kaufingerstraße 24, 80331 München, Germany